Advance

"*If a book could be compared to a magic lantern, this work of Dr. Susan R. Meyer would be it. This book keeps on giving through each chapter. It's filled with insights that really support decision-making and your heart's desires. Dr. Meyer has a genius understanding of life, career choices, and overcoming obstacles. She has her finger on the pulse of change and speaks from her own experiences and a deep wisdom of the journey of others. I am keeping my copy nearby. It's a wish fulfiller.*"

~Phyllis Haynes, Global speaker, coach, producer, ABC broadcast journalist and host of *Straight Talk*

"*Dr. Susan Meyer provides doable exercises, steps and strategies to help you find your true career path so that you can become the master of your own fate, just as she has!*"

~Lori Sokol, Ph.D., Executive Director/Editor-in-Chief, Women's eNews, award winning author of *She is Me*

"*Negotiating successful careers is based on knowing how to weather transitions and growing and learning from each experience no matter how difficult. Susan's book clearly presents a path forward based on real experience, extensive education and expertise in learning and change, combined with many concrete strategies and tools. Her humor is delightful and inspirational. I immediately ordered copies for my daughter and nephew. Relevant no matter what age.*"

~Dr. Ann L. Clancy, transformational coach and author of *Appreciative Coaching: A Positive Process for Change and Pivoting: A Coach's Guide to Igniting Substantial Change*

I'M SUSAN

AND I'M A
SERIAL CAREERIST

Seven Success Strategies
for a Unique Career

Dr. Susan R. Meyer

The Three Tomatoes Book Publishing

Published January 2022
ISBN: 978-1-7376177-8-5
Library of Congress Control Number: 9781737617785

For information address:
The Three Tomatoes Book Publishing
6 Soundview Rd.
Glen Cove, NY 11542

Cover design: Susan Herbst
Cover Illustration: runeer
Interior design: Susan Herbst

Dedication

*This book is dedicated to everyone who has ever found themselves lost in
their own life plan,
And to three who found their way and left us too soon:
Louise Lauro Meyer
Kelly Ann Lynch
Marsha Lehman*

Forward

"Sometimes when I consider what tremendous consequences come from little things, I am tempted to think... there are no little things."

~ Bruce Barton

Edward Lorenz's butterfly effect tells us that if you make even a tiny change in one variable, over time, you will get radically different results. When we plot those changes, we notice that they don't tend to go back to the original starting point. If you set three bodies – a pendulum or a career – into motion at the same time, they will only move together for a short time, then they will diverge from one another. Tiny changes or shifts in our careers can make the future unpredictable... yet it will unfold beautifully into an image of a butterfly.

Dr. Susan Meyer's personal story – her unfolding butterfly - is punched up with insights and pearls of wisdom that can only be gathered looking backward at the patterns that begin presenting themselves. Her personal experiences, shared in story form, add color to the principles. They also make it evident that you are not alone!

The skills she learned in eighth grade to increase the flexibility of her wardrobe are at the center of how she has set up the sections of this book: Start with what you have. Then add pieces a few at a time so you can mix and match knowledge and skills in creative and authentic ways, so that you can refresh your take on what's possible for you.

This book is filled with pearls of wisdom, all hard-earned and beautifully shared by a professional whose work I admire. Dr. Susan is very forthright in her storytelling – vulnerable and authentic – and freely offers the tools and perspectives that life gave her along her journey so you and I can choose to build from them.

Written with the sensibilities of a teacher, mentor and coach, the activities and exercises in this book are thought-provoking and helpful to gaining clarity of thought and emotion. Like her eighth-grade wardrobe-building experience, she invites the learner to start with what he/she/they have, add pieces and insights that coordinate, creating a unique understanding of what's possible for the reader.

For me, the shift from craving recognition to carving meaning came after a serious health crisis. The desire to find and express whole-life satisfaction truly resonates with me and has for a while. The idea of building a possible new career – or, at the very least, a new direction – is genuinely appealing. Refreshing my understanding of what I know and do well, expanding my network of relationships and reassessing my priorities and the direction(s) in which I focus my attention. All are ways for me to stretch my thinking and to see new possibilities available to me.

It is always a great strategy to walk intentionally toward your fear. And there may be no one whose wisdom I trust more to guide me than Dr. Susan. She has the academic and real-life background, as well as a touch of magic in her approaches. Further, her years in coaching and coach development are evident in the gentle, yet robust way she encourages the reader to think about and apply the learning she offers. I especially appreciate the "Experiment and Document" exercises, inviting the reader to think of themselves as more of a scientist than a someone merely floating along in life.

This book is an excellent resource for individuals who are ready to get serious about what is (still) possible for them! It also lends itself nicely to small group discussion or coaching work. I am glad to add this book to my library of resources to share with family, friends, and clients.

Dr. Lucía Murphy, aka "Doctor Murph"
Managing principal
The Leadership Architect Group

Table of Contents

Introduction

There's a whole new idea of what a career looks like. Gone are the days when a career was considered staying with one organization straight through to retirement, maybe changing departments once or twice, maybe getting a couple of promotions. In fact, that notion of a career has never been true for many people – especially women – for decades. An ever-increasing number of people leap from rock to rock in the career stream, some with a plan and purpose, others just hoping for the best. They explore new opportunities and often take time off for relaxation or adventures.

Have you had a series of work experiences, volunteer experiences, independent ventures, careers that you haven't quite seen as a pattern? Have you moved through a series of jobs, volunteer gigs, life experiences, and fallow periods? Has your paid employment trajectory been interrupted by other life experiences like travel, child rearing, illness, caregiving? You might be what I call a non-sequential or serial careerist. To an outsider, your career may look like chaos. They don't understand that this is a loosely organized pattern. It may be that you don't quite get it yourself yet. You know what you want; you simply haven't figured out the path toward those goals.

Are you ready to learn how to use all that you are, all that you know, and all that you've done to find your steppingstones and create a clear path for your future? The seven strategies in this book, presented with parts of my story and the stories of people I've interviewed or coached, provide a context for each strategy.

For more than five decades I've moved through a series of varied work experiences – eighteen different full-time jobs, plus summer jobs, part-time jobs, temp work, three periods as an independent consultant, a couple of attempts at full retirement, and a few dry spells where I couldn't figure out what was next.

This seemed like an unusual path in the late '60s. Most men stayed in one career – often, one workplace – their entire work life. Many women were homemakers and volunteers or worked outside the home part-time while their children were young or part- or full-time after their children were grown. Some who had full-time jobs while raising children did so out of economic necessity. Another group had "disrupted" careers, taking time off for childbirth, still often staying in the same field their entire careers, and another segment followed the same path as most men, staying with one organization for their entire work life. It's only in the last few years that many women have increasingly become the largest group of new entrepreneurs.

For millennials and beyond, it's much more common to have a non-sequential or serial career. An increasing number of people in these groups drop out of the workforce periodically and change jobs or careers as their interests drive them. They follow their passions instead of working their way up a corporate ladder. This book is for people like me who may be looking back at their own zigzag path, wondering what's next. It's for people whose careers have been disrupted for any reason or who now have responsibilities or limitations that force them to change direction. It's for women and men who, in their forties and beyond, are dissatisfied with their current life and want something new – whether that's moving into the world of work, changing direction, or building meaning and purpose into retirement.

It's for younger workers who want to deliberately create their own serial career and who would like a few signposts for the road ahead.

I've divided serial careerists into three groups with specific tips and advice for each group in each chapter to make it easier for you to see what's most applicable to your life and how you might make the exercises more personal. Here are the groups:

Curious and Restless

Several women that I interviewed added "easily bored" to this description. I'm finding this to be increasing as more people are seeing a career as a series of challenges and as the notion of lifelong loyalty to one employer diminishes. Many people who saw their parents lose everything – or who themselves lost everything – in the '80s fit into this category. Their loyalty is to themselves and, while they will give their all to each position, they will rarely stay once there's no challenge or the position interferes with their overall lifestyle and well-being. People in this group are not necessarily planners. It's a good habit to develop, though, if only to track your progress and steer clear of past pitfalls.

Mid-career to Near Retirement

This group may have stayed in one position for many years. At some point, generally at midlife, they have started to shift from craving recognition and achievement to craving meaning in their lives. They may be feeling stuck or blocked from increased responsibility. They are focused on whole-life satisfaction. Those in this group will benefit from a thorough skills analysis as well as experimenting with new career possibilities.

Re-entry or Late Entry

This group includes those who have been homemakers and/or caregivers for extended periods of time. It also includes those who have experienced a significant life change (divorce, loss of a spouse or partner, empty nest) and desire or are forced to find a career. They will benefit from all the strategies and may want to begin with visioning.

If any of this sounds like you, if you're thinking about managing your own serial career or simply restarting or changing your career, you'll find, mixed into my own story, strategies, tips, and ways to avoid potential pitfalls along the way. It's based on my journey and my experience as a Life Architect and Career Strategist. It's about the starts, false starts, and stops, the successes, an occasional miracle, and a few blind alleys.

Your journey will be different, though the fundamentals will be remarkably similar for everyone on this path. Make sure that you're equipped to make your journey a glorious adventure. Although careers have become much more fluid, there are still underlying organizing principles. I've probably made every mistake in the book along the way, so consider doing what I say, not what I did. You'll find plenty of new wrong turns or stumbles to make on your own.

The strategies here are not meant to be one-time or one size fits all. If you review them each time you come to a decision point, refining them as needed to fit your personal journey, you'll be making more informed decisions about the direction your life takes. You may still have false starts. You may still make mistakes – but they'll be informed mistakes. If you see what led you to a decision, you'll more clearly see how to do a course correction. If you fly blindly, well, as Yogi Berra may have said, "If you see a fork in the road, take it," and take your chances.

The seven strategies plus tips and exercises are presented within the framework of the chronology of my life story so that you can easily see examples of how they apply to specific life decisions. This is followed by a longer version of my life history with insights integrated. Next is a recap of the strategies and exercises for easy reference because I hate hunting through a book to find something when I need it. Finally, there are a few general thoughts about the lifetime process of following a unique career path and some additional resources.

The strategies:

- **Explore your life.**

Take time to document your roots as well as your work history. This will help you identify your values, your strengths, and your potential obstacles or stumbling blocks and to see how these may be rooted in your family history. The information will help you make more informed choices.

- **Know your skills and challenges.**

Whether you do a full analysis or make a list, knowing what you can – and like to – do helps you expand your thinking beyond work similar to what you've already done and to explore new possibilities. It also helps you identify things that you find difficult so that you can clearly identify potential trade-offs or compromises.

- **Maintain and expand relationships.**

We all need a strong support network. Identify yours. Periodically check and update your family and friendship circles.

- **Recombine skills.**

There are so any different ways to use your skills! A consultant who went from working with people with substance abuse issues to young entrepreneurs was not surprised that both groups relied on the same core skills. Think about skill clusters before you focus on specific jobs. Look at how your skills fit together in unexpected ways.

- **Be patient; experiment and stay open to miracles and new possibilities.**

Experiment, tell everyone what you're looking for, and ask a lot of questions. Expect the unusual. Say yes more often. Be surprised!

• Deal with fear.

This doesn't mean putting yourself in danger. It means stretching. It means not holding back out of fear of failure. There are good outcomes to be had from mistakes.

• Reassess; reprioritize.

Over time, your skill set changes. Some are so rusty from disuse that you may never bring them back to their original luster. A few have become obsolete. Some that you once loved you may never want to use again. Examine what may be holding you back.

Even if you're not looking for change in the moment, periodically update your skills inventory, your support network, your finances, and your deepest dreams. Although I'd recommend starting with the first two strategies so that you have a base of knowledge about yourself, feel free to head straight for what calls to you. Jump around. Go back and forth. Do the same exercise multiple times. Please remember that the successes and difficulties you'll read about are someone else's. The exact same circumstances might play out very differently for you. Above all, enjoy the journey. Bon voyage!

Chapter 1

Exploring Your Roots

Even though "the apple doesn't fall far from the tree" is a cliché, there's still a lot of truth in the statement. Or maybe not. It's important for you to know how your roots and your early experiences can shape your choices. For example, I'm not just bad at math, I'm downright math-phobic. I can trace the roots of this deficit to two events. First, a change of schools meant that I was behind everyone else in arithmetic. My class was well into multiplication while I had barely mastered addition and subtraction. I didn't have a clue. Second, my aunt taught me the times tables using the wooden spoon method. If I got the answer right, I did NOT get hit over the head with her wooden spoon. Ask me to multiply today and I'm still likely to wince and duck.

The overview of my life up until college is followed by a list of skills and potential issues that I can trace to my pre-college life. This is not meant to tell you more about me than you really want to know but rather to demonstrate the potential connections between your past and your future and to help you think about writing a similar history.

There are lessons and skills learned in your early childhood that may get you through the worst of times. There may be other lessons that will always be demons. List and remember your core strengths. List and address the demons. Your strengths and your demons will be part of every choice you ever make. You may need to decide how much pain or discomfort you are willing to take on in order to do something that you are passionate about.

My Background: Roots and Early Years

I see my life as a series of contradictions and a constant balancing act. I consider myself to be both a very successful professional and an underachiever. I am the product of at least two generations of contradiction and conflict, so I come by it naturally. In this chapter I provide an extensive look at my life before I began my career. For me, it was important to look at the roots of the skills and assets that are the underpinnings of my choices as well as the origins of those that grew out of painful experiences. I needed to see these patterns to understand not only my past decisions but also what to consider as I make new choices.

My paternal grandparents were an odd combination. My grandmother always said her parents were British. Decades later we found out that they were actually Prussian Jews who spent a brief time in England and that my great-grandparents were actually born in Toronto and Kansas City. The fiction remained, though. Her father, a jeweler, was the poor relation of an upper-middle-class family. They had only one servant. As near as I can tell, his wife was a professional invalid.

My grandmother completed high school – unusual in 1918 - and went on to the Katherine Gibbs Secretarial School. She was an executive secretary most of her life. To the day she retired, she wore white gloves to work and prided herself on being the fastest and most accurate typist in the organization. My great-aunt worked in the music store her husband owned and was reputed to be the first woman to be accepted into the Pianoforte Tuners' Association. Both worked most of their adult lives, my grandmother until retirement and my great-aunt until arthritis made tuning impossible, so there's a precedent for working women on that side.

My grandmother's parents were stereotypically reserved Brits. They weren't warm with their children and didn't praise them. No one ever praised my grandmother while she was growing up; no one ever told her that she was smart; no one ever told her that she was pretty; so when a handsome young man climbed over the seat in a movie theater and told her she was beautiful she married him. There's a long history of not feeling good enough. Gram overcompensated by being brash.

My grandfather's family, by contrast, were lower-class Germans. He managed to finish third grade before becoming a bricklayer. His father was an upholsterer and his mother cleaned houses. Mostly, though, his family drank. My only memory of my great-grandfather is of him sitting in a big, wingback chair asking for another beer. My grandfather was handsome and charming right up to the point where he became drunk, loud, and mean. Although he had been a foreman and was sent to Bermuda to build military installations, he aged out of his construction career as building construction changed. He went through a series of jobs that relied on his natural charm, including selling novelty advertising items (cocktail napkins, matchbooks) to businesses. He bred exotic fish and was a fixture at pet shows. With my grandmother's help, he wrote articles about breeding fish. Somehow, my grandparents managed to stay married, survive the Depression, and raise three sons to adulthood.

My maternal grandparents were second-generation Italian immigrants. I don't know much about them; they were atypically not given to either communication or family gatherings. My great-grandmother put all her sons' names in a hat, the legend goes, and drew the name of the one son that all the other children (male and female) would work to put through college. My grandfather was the lucky winner and eventually completed both a law degree and a doctorate in chemistry. His first wife, his childhood sweetheart, died of tuberculosis, shortly before her thirtieth birthday, when my mother was nine years old. This left her with lifelong scars that carried over to affect me.

His second wife, who had been his housekeeper, transformed herself from German hausfrau to the perfect Italian wife to please my grandfather, but he never stopped talking about his first wife, whom we started calling "the blessed sainted Mary," and his son and daughter never accepted their stepmother.

My parents met while working on their high school literary magazine. When my dad was accepted to the Agriculture School at Cornell, my mother followed him there. Mom was supposed to study chemistry and fulfill her father's desire to set her up with her own analysis business. She had other ideas, mainly to not let my father out of her sight. Dad's plan was to be a writer, not a farmer. Their plans were disrupted by World War II. They had a small wedding before he shipped out to Europe and managed to create me during a weekend leave in Madison, Wisconsin. Mom never went back to class, but Dad finished college when the war ended. The college converted what may have been chicken coops into Vetsburg, housing for all the veteran families, and there we lived until Dad graduated. My mother had a small circle of devoted friends who helped care for me while my father was overseas.

After Dad completed school, we moved around a few times before settling in Hatboro, not far from Philadelphia. He became a technical writer. For the next few years, I had an idyllic childhood, with a small close-knit group of neighborhood children to play with, art lessons, Brownie Scouts, a big, beautiful collie, and, when I was seven, a baby brother.

Those years in Hatboro saved me by getting me off to a good start. They established a core of strength and independence. I felt loved. I was a free spirit, a leader and an artist. I had yet to know loss or fear. I loved and trusted my parents. I had that same level of trust for all the adults in my life. As I got older and things fell apart, I learned about pain and meanness and untrustworthy people. I withdrew and hid. I felt like everything that was wrong was my fault. But still, somewhere in there was that core of strength and the memory of that little girl, and I know it helped me survive and eventually heal.

Shortly after my brother's birth, we moved to a townhouse in a more urban area near Newark, New Jersey. Starting with that move from Pennsylvania to New Jersey, I started to feel like an outsider. Moving so many times meant a series of adjustments – learning how to get along with new kids, trying to figure out what was going on in school. Kids are the harshest critics and don't take kindly to anything that is even a little different. The new kid always stands out, and if there's anything different about that kid, it becomes (or feels like it becomes) almost impossible to fit in.

The move to New Jersey was an uncomfortable transition for me. My parents put me in a Catholic school. Being the only non-Catholic in my first school in New Jersey made fitting in hard. I'd never even seen a nun before and now my world was ruled by them. I had never been inside a Catholic church.

I did not understand any of the catechism we were required to learn. The subjects were different. Worst of all, soon after we moved, my mother became ill. I was the only child with a sick mother, the only child with a housekeeper, the only one who hadn't learned the Palmer method or the times tables. The only thing I did well was reading. And still, I often got in trouble because I read so fast that I was always ahead of my group. More than once, I got put into the slow group because Sister Martin Elizabeth never realized that I was a chapter ahead.

This was the beginning of a pattern of uncomfortable transitions. I learned early to be quiet and stay in the background for as long as I could. I was always trying to fit in and never quite figuring it out. I went from being the ringleader to the shy kid in the corner. It wasn't in me to be a follower, so I was most often an outsider. It was a pattern that stayed with me through most of my life.

No one told me what was going on with my mother, or how ill she really was. The house became a place of hushed whispers and silences. Doctors came and went. I couldn't figure out what was going on and learned, for the first time, that adults withheld information. This left me always seeking information, always wanting to know what was going on.

When my mother was hospitalized and my father felt he could not keep up with all the demands of work and parenting, we moved in with his brother and sister-in-law on Long Island. We remained there for about a year after my mother died. My mother, like her mother, died shortly before her thirtieth birthday, also leaving a son and a daughter. Like my mother, I was just short of nine years old. I was convinced that I too would die before my thirtieth birthday. I didn't do a lot of long-range planning until after my thirtieth birthday.

By the time I was nine (when we moved into my aunt's house) I had become increasingly insecure about myself. That self-confident leader from my Hatboro days was shaken by the changes that were going on and, with no one to talk to about any of this, I began to assume that it was all my fault. That there was something wrong with me. That no one really cared about me and it was because of some flaw within me. Maybe it was my fault that my mother was so sick. This insecurity still comes back, no matter how I've worked on it, no matter how successful I've been. It seems that some of us need constant reminders.

My aunt's house was the center of her family and the center of the neighborhood. The fathers weren't around much. My uncle was working and getting his engineering degree at night and my father was still living in New Jersey during the week. The house was always full of children – my two cousins, my brother and me, my aunt's sister's children, and seemingly every kid in a four-block radius. Whenever I could get away with it, I took refuge in the garage, where our old furniture was stored, and read in peace. Although my aunt was very social, I was not. She assumed that I was just stubborn and could fit in with the other kids.

After we moved in with my aunt, this feeling of not fitting in got worse. Everyone else had two parents at home; my father was only around weekends and my mother was in the hospital. Clearly, I was weird. I became weirder when Mom died and I was the only child with only one parent. No one had any idea about how to deal with a grieving child. No one talked to me about my loss, and it seemed that I was expected to just forget about my mother. At some point, I developed what they called a "nervous stomach" and was prescribed a nerve tonic. That was the only acknowledgment of what I was going through. I don't think that anyone in the neighborhood had lost a parent when they were a child, so there was no frame of reference to fall back on. I'm not sure if therapy for children even existed.

I had a whole collection of books that my grandfather had given to my mother. The heroines were always strong, independent orphan girls who made good and/or rescued their relatives from some plight. I modeled myself after these girls and it's been a sub-theme for many of my career choices. I always was counter-authoritarian. I always preferred the underdog. Lots of mothers told their daughters that it was just as easy to marry a rich man as a poor man. My coaches told me that it was just as easy to coach rich clients as poor ones. I wasn't buying any of it.

I was packed off to summer camp, where I learned how to ride and swim and developed an interest in crafts. It was a welcome change and allowed me enough freedom to be more like my old self. It was this YWCA camp where I first became friends with children from other religions, races, and cultures. It was also where I learned a bunch of "Native American" songs that on closer inspection turned out to be Hebrew folk songs.

About a year after we moved in with my aunt, my father came back from a conference in California and announced that he was getting married. She was the only woman in an engineering firm and had always wanted to get married to validate her femininity. He wanted a mother for his two children. Although everything I knew about step-mothers I'd learned in fairy tales, I wanted this woman to love me and tried as hard as I could to earn her acceptance, split between a need for love and feeling disloyal to and missing my mother.

What I didn't realize was this woman knew nothing about children or parenting and her own mother had raised her to be cold and distant. We were doomed from the start. Dad and I flew to California for the wedding and, tucked into a sort of shelf on the back of the MG, I accompanied them on their honeymoon – the drive back to New York.

Shortly before my tenth birthday, I became the built-in babysitter for my brother, and a part-time housekeeper. I remember spending a lot of time polishing my stepmother's copper-bottomed pots. I don't remember much of this period. I don't remember having any friends or doing anything but going to school, coming home, and cleaning.

Within a year, Edith came to hate the East Coast and decided to move back to California. We settled into the San Fernando Valley. I had never seen anything like my school there! It was a series of pink stucco buildings. I liked school and was more popular than I'd ever been before – being an Easterner made me instantly perceived as smart and sophisticated.

While school got better, things at home got worse. My stepmother was quickly adding physical abuse to verbal abuse. On weekends, most of the time I was charged with taking my brother with me to a neighborhood park. We'd pick up bottles along the roadside to cash in for enough to buy candy.

The physical abuse that Edith inflicted had two effects. It made me often hit my brother when he wasn't behaving, mimicking what was happening to me. I felt guilty but couldn't completely stop. Also, I sometimes had marks from Edith's beatings. She would sit on my back and beat me until her arms were tired or tell my father I'd done something wrong and make him hit me with his belt. I felt like it was my fault. No matter how hard I tried to please Edith I never could, and since my father never defended me, what she said about me must have been true.

The summer I turned twelve, my grandparents came out to visit. My stepmother apparently convinced them that they needed a lasting memento of their visit, because I was shipped off to live with them. Returning to the East Coast to enter eighth grade was a disaster. West Coast transfer students were considered to be behind their East Coast peers, so I was put into the slowest of the eighth grade classes. My teacher admitted to realizing immediately that this was a mistake, but she was so thrilled to have one bright child in her class that she did nothing about the situation. I felt uncomfortable as the class star.

My stepmother had also spent the last year I lived with her convincing me that I was fat – an image I've held and lived up to most of my life. When I moved back east, puberty hit, and I actually started putting on weight. This made me the brunt of jokes by some of my classmates through high school. It was just one more thing that made me feel unpopular, unimportant, and a failure.

Although my grandmother was indulgent, she was also distant. My grandfather's alcoholism was getting more and more out of hand. He was verbally abusive to my grandmother and sometimes physically abusive. Although he was loving when he was sober, he was rarely sober for long and often pinned me down and threatened me. I was terrified of him.

Since I had returned to the neighborhood where my parents had grown up, I went to the same high school they had attended. Because I had been in a lower class in eighth grade, I was tracked into a lower class in high school, and it took me a year to get moved into an honors section – the top two classes. I was luckier than in eighth grade. Because the principal had fond memories of my father, who had been extraordinarily popular, he looked out for me. Finally, I was able to take pride in being smart and doing well in school.

During mid-term week my freshman year, I went home for lunch between tests to find out that my father had been killed in a car accident. This is the first time I consciously remember using humor to get through a situation. I went back to school to take my second test of the day, but I made my girlfriend tell me every joke she knew to get me through the experience.

Perhaps because I felt like I'd lost him when I was sent to live with my grandparents, I weathered my father's death better than my mother's. I took refuge in school and school activities, and, despite a weight problem, managed to have a boyfriend of sorts. I was an editor of the literary magazine, a class officer, one of the major organizers of our senior variety show, and part of the most active, popular group in the school, but I never realized my own power. I continued to feel like an outsider and guilty about some unspecified dirty secret. Few outsiders ever got past the seeming normalcy of my grandparents' home to see what really went on.

The pattern of combined over-achievement and low self-esteem that I developed early in life was compounded and underscored by similar patterns I had learned from my family. I always had to be doing more and I never felt I was doing well enough. I never believed any evidence of my own successes. No place, except deep in the pages of a book, was really safe. It was important to try to please everyone and stay as close to invisible as possible if you didn't want pain – emotional and sometimes physical. It was important to hide a lot of my life. It was important to stop and observe to figure out how to fit in.

What's important for you in this part of my story?

What does this have to do with being a serial careerist? The lessons of my childhood shaped the adult I became. The better I understood my baggage, the better decisions I was able to make. I learned which of my issues I could deal with, which actually made me better at certain kinds of work, and which required big trade-offs if I was to succeed. The same is true for you.

Based on your family history and early experiences, some of your choices may require doing things that are hard for you. You may have to decide how much discomfort or pain you can deal with to realize your passions. I've chosen a path that requires extraversion in my professional life. I've found that possible because being with people is the primary path I've chosen to help them. The teaching and coaching have been wonderful. On the other hand, my self-doubts have consistently left me great at marketing others yet not good at marketing myself. Because of that, I've primarily chosen paths where someone else would market me.

Have your family and cultural influences limited or expanded your choices? How? Are there things that you were afraid to try or things that you felt compelled to do whether or not you wanted to? The more you know about what informed your choices, the better your future choices are likely to be.

Strategy 1: Explore Your Roots

Exercise: Family History

It helps to understand your past as you consider your future. It took me a long time to recognize the patterns that hold me back and those that help me move forward. Take some time to look back at your family journey. Document it. You'll find detailed instructions in Chapter 9.

Why should you write a life history? When I was teaching Career Development I discovered the magic of Life History and began using it with my classes. Write your history. Be as thorough as you can. I recommend doing this in two rounds. In the first round, get down as many facts as you can. In the second round, flesh out the document with stories and feelings. Look for patterns. How do these patterns influence your life choices? What are your coping mechanisms? Do they serve you well or would you like to change them?

Life is made up of a series of building blocks. These blocks represent the relationship between our experiences and our belief system. We pile these blocks one on top of the other to create the pattern that is our lives. Sometimes, though, the pattern is not what we expected.

When a bricklayer constructs a wall, he carefully examines his materials. He looks over each brick to be sure that it is true – no cracks, not warped in any way, of the same color and construction as the other bricks that will make up the wall. Then he carefully mixes the ingredients to make the mortar that will hold the bricks together. If the ingredients are not in balance, the mortar will be too thin and not hold or will dry and crack. The bricks will not stay in place. Carefully, very carefully, the bricklayer puts just the right amount of mortar on the trowel, then gently taps the brick in place, smoothing away the excess, making sure the brick is aligned with the others – not too far forward, not too far back. If only we could build the walls of our own lives with such care!

Unfortunately, we don't have this luxury. Our lives develop – often without much attention. Some of the bricks may be faulty. Some may really be bars of gold. In examining our life histories, we are, in effect, looking at each of the bricks in our walls. Some may be excellent; some may need to be replaced. Part of the work you will be doing is reviewing the basic constructs – the bricks – that make up your life to date. This experience may be exhilarating or painful or both. By the time you have finished, you will have a clearer picture of who you are and what basic thoughts or underlying assumptions have governed the decisions you have made to date. If you find your story painful, consider working with a coach or a therapist who can help you face the tough bits and understand how to accept and move beyond the pain.

It also helps to document all of your skills. This is especially important for a serial careerist because you are relying on our transferable skills – and you never know what will turn out to be useful. For example, who knew that handling things that others considered disgusting could shift someone else's perspective?

A participant in a career prep program I was leading was just going through the motions. She was apathetic. She was depressed. After much prodding, I discovered that she liked caring for animals and got her an internship at the Bronx Zoo. She showed up, but nothing changed. Then, one day she was asked to feed a mouse to a snake. Many of us would run screaming. She loved it. She reported back to the group overjoyed. She was a different woman. She pushed to finish her application and got into college and completed her degree in biology and is still happily employed at the zoo.

A less strange, yet unusual example is Gloria, a fifty-year-old woman who was getting her associate's degree so that she could work as a teacher's aide. After she completed her skills analysis, she discovered that the same skills – communication, leadership, and persuasion – that made her successful in the classroom were transferable to politics. She decided to explore this career option. She got elected to the community board and went on to a seat in the state assembly.

What are you good at? What do you love? What is difficult for you? What do you hate? How can you recombine or reframe or recycle your skills to fit the career choices you want to make? You'll find detailed instructions on this and the exercises in other chapters and in chapter 9.

Where do we go from here?
The chapters that follow include pitfalls you might want to avoid, exercises that could be useful in better understanding yourself and in making decisions. You'll also see how skills can be transferred, recycled, blended, and used in unexpected ways.

I've been a serial careerist since I was twenty, although I realize that I've never strayed very far from my overarching passion – to teach. I know that teaching, in some form, was always by choice, but I'll never be sure about some of my choices along the way because options for women overall were far fewer. The field of technology barely existed. Computers were giant machines (see the movie *Desk Set* to see them in action), and programming involved a huge stack of cards with ones and zeros. You dropped them at your own peril. There were no cell phones. We used carbon paper or rexograph machines if we needed copies. No one had even conceived of an internet, much less the apps that crowd our phones and tablets today. Teaching was confined to classrooms. Health care had not yet expanded to include so many modalities and options like physician assistants or computerized medical records or a proliferation of home health care and training programs for all these fields.

When I graduated, there were a handful of choices that I knew about for English majors. Most families pushed their daughters to teach because that way they'd have summers off and have a schedule that roughly corresponded to their children's once they became mothers. Editorial assistant was a coveted choice. If you typed really well, you might earn $6,000 a year. I failed the typing test and couldn't even get hired by McGraw Hill, where my father had worked. Working for Time-Life was another option. I don't know what the real title was, but we called them "clippers." The job consisted of clipping articles from newspapers and magazines to be filed away and retrieved for whenever reporters needed information.

Teaching jobs may have been secure, but they were nearly impossible to get – waiting lists could be a year or more. That left a couple of civil service options. The two I knew about were caseworker for the City's Social Services Department or employment development specialist for the State Employment Service. The State paid $100 more a year – the grand sum of $6,500 – so that's what I picked. Probably not the best reason for a career decision.

As you reflect on your own trajectory, your struggles, and your successes, it's my hope that my story and those of others I've interviewed will help you recognize consistent threads and patterns in your own life and how to use them to create and sustain the life you want. To help you do this, there are strategies and exercises scattered along the path and summarized at the end of the book.

Many books about creating a better life are, in part, autobiographical. The general idea is "do what I did." This one is a little different. As I tell audiences, I've made every mistake in the book. Please, do what I suggest only if it works for you. Find your own mistakes! It pretty much never feels like it in the moment, but mistakes are often our best teachers.

At worst, you'll have a lot of great stories. At best, you'll open avenues you've never considered. There's a lot of serendipity in our mistakes. You'll also have a better idea of what shaped the way you see yourself.

Dr. Susan R. Meyer

Chapter 2

Know What You Know

Being a successful serial careerist involves organization and planning even when your specific decisions may appear random and may be spontaneous. A plan gives you something to fall back on. A great plan is one that you can abandon, revise, and return to. There are two parts to creating a great plan. One is having an overall vision of what you want out of life accompanied by a set of goals that may be very fluid. The other part is knowing what you have to work with at any time – your skills, your preferences, your assets, your liabilities, and your finances. In this chapter, we'll focus on the skills area. Knowing what skills you have and prefer may influence your vision and goals.

I spent several decades in jobs that were either teaching or helping others without seeing any pattern. At fifty, I knew that my job was killing me and just quit – no plan, few resources, just a lot of hope. There are better ways to do this. There's a quote that says, "When you reach the end of all you know and leap you will have wings to fly." I believe that. I've always said that when I have one foot off the cliff and the other on a banana peel a miracle always happens. I've been lucky, but not always smart. If you can be both, you'll be much better off.

So what made me decide at fifty that I was going to strike out on my own? I'd tried twice before to set up my own coaching and consulting business, with no success. Why would this time be different? Motivation. I knew I couldn't spend one more day in that job. I was miserable and convinced that the job was damaging my physical and mental health. It wasn't worth fifteen more years of misery to ensure a healthy pension. So I leapt. And lived to tell the tale.

As a doctoral student I discovered that there's something called reflected self-concept. Some people only see themselves in what they see reflected by others – bad or good, true or false. They have no internal grounding. Over time, I have worked with clients who have exactly this issue and find myself momentarily sucked in and reliving my own trauma while we work on theirs; each session becomes a reminder to reset my own internal grounding mechanism.

I've read that by age five our personalities are set, so I feel like at least I have a sound base to fall back on, but it takes a lot of work and constant attention to separate out lingering false beliefs from reality. If this is an issue for you, the work of coach Byron Katie, author of many books including *Loving What Is* and *The Work*, is helpful. Her core question – "Is that true?" – is an excellent entry into clearing false beliefs and re-grounding yourself.

It wasn't until recently that I chronicled my high school and college years. I had a clearer picture of the origins of my weaknesses and ambivalences from reviewing my family roots and early years, and I realized that it was important to also take a deeper look at my strengths and identify the skills I developed in high school and college. These skills determined many of my career choices and were useful in finding interim employment. The inventory of those skills also made it very clear what I can and can't do.

For example, one challenge in high school was having a great wardrobe on a limited budget. Every semester, my best friend and I had a fifty-dollar clothing allowance. The challenge was to put together as many combinations as possible to never wear the same outfit twice in a two-week period. We got very good at this mix-and-match concept. The challenge was to see how much money we'd have left over. If we did a pretty good job, we'd have fries and cherry lime rickeys at the bus depot. If we did really well, it was hamburgers and hot fudge sundaes. This wardrobe planning skill still serves me well. I can still tell you every piece of clothing I own and every other item it goes with. I've taken over the management of some friends' closets.

Thanks to my grandfather, who was head chemist at the NY Produce Exchange Bureau of Chemistry, I got my first full-time summer job as a clerk there. The Bureau tested products traded on the Exchange and cereal for the NY State prisons. Actually, the chemists took the cereal home and I was tasked with creating the reports (the chemists ate the cereal) and typing them in quadruplicate – which meant three carbon copies. Working with carbon paper was a nightmare if you were a bad typist because a solution had to be applied to each sheet of carbon paper if you needed to make a correction. I quickly discovered that I was not a good typist. That summer taught me that I never wanted to be a clerk. On the plus side, the secretary taught me how to walk more like a lady than a truck driver and introduced me to discount stores that helped me upgrade my wardrobe on almost no money.

My desire to become a teacher created a couple of interesting academic non-choices in high school. When it came time to choose a language, we were asked who wanted to be a teacher and everyone who raised their hand was conscripted into Latin. I suppose that three and a half years of Latin and a semester of Greek did improve my vocabulary. The second time I foolishly raised my hand I ended up taking Public Speaking. I hated it. If the teacher liked us, he signed us up for a second semester. I hated it twice. I never wanted to have to get up in front of a group and speak. Still, everything I learned came back to me decades later when I started training City employees.

When I was ready to go to college, I knew that I couldn't stay home. I applied to the State University at Albany. I fell in love with it the minute I saw the place. This was '63 so we were beginning to get political in New York City, but politics hadn't really hit upstate in the same way they hit downstate. There were as many students from New York City and Long Island as from Albany and upstate New York, so it was normal for there to be a lot of diversity of opinion. There were few people of color other than a handful of foreign students, and no openly gay students. We were, for the most part, united in our naivete. There was generally a rift, as there still is within the state, between upstate and downstate.

When I left home, a whole different world opened up to me. I loved college. I had a double major in English and Comparative Literature and an Education minor at that point and I was preparing to teach high school English because, after all, I had always loved English and I wrote in high school. Away from my family, I could be whomever I wanted to be. I had been dieting the summer before and didn't feel too out of place (i.e., fat). I discovered diet pills, and every month one of my closest friends and I would take the bus to the city to get our supply. I managed to remain thin for most of my college years.

Most of my college experience continued in a pattern of conflicting interests and experiences – moving from a carefree existence to national tragedy, from optimism to pessimism. I worked on an underground newsletter yet rushed a sorority. My friends were beatniks and conservatives, Greeks and Independents.

I was sure that I'd be a teacher right up until I got to student teaching. I discovered very quickly that I had no sense of discipline or class control and had trouble managing the elite eighth-graders in the campus school. I really had a hard time controlling the class, but I had a wonderful mentor who taught reading and he got me interested in being a Remedial Reading teacher.

The main campus was surrounded by Albany High School and the annex to Albany High School. We would walk down the block and very tall teenagers would sort of come up behind us and somehow kick snow over our heads and into our faces. This, combined with my student teaching experience, gave me a clue that maybe high school students would be a bigger challenge than I'd imagined. Still, I graduated and left Albany without any clear idea of what would happen next, buoyed by the naiveté of youth and without a plan. If I knew about creating a skills list, I might have had a better idea.

What's important for you in this part of my story?

I jumped into the world of work without any forethought or planning. I had no knowledge of what my vision was beyond wanting to teach. I hadn't researched. I didn't really have goals. While this is true of many people, you can save a lot of time by understanding yourself and doing some planning. This will eliminate a number of false starts and wrong directions.

Documenting your skills and updating the list periodically keeps you open to possibilities and alternatives. Knowing your core values enhances your decision-making process. Even though your overall vision and mission may change – or at least become more refined over time – they will work in tandem with your values to give you an overall sense of direction. Knowing what you want to do and what you're best at, knowing what won't work for you, helps you remain realistic yet also improves your ability to reimagine your dream job.

For the curious and restless group: Think about your skills list as a marvelous grab bag. You can reach in and take out a handful of skills to pick a few for your next adventure.

For the mid-career/pre-retirement group: You may have come to a point where you no longer want to rely on the core skills that have gotten you this far. Having a skills list gives you a good base for identifying skills you would prefer to use and for helping you find a new direction.

For the late-entry or re-entry group: This exercise is a real confidence-builder. It's an opportunity to see how many of the skills you've used outside of paid employment translate into job skills.

For all groups: vision, mission, and values are your compass.

Strategy 2: Know Your Skills and Challenges

Exercises

These exercises will help you get a clear picture of your skills, strengths, and potential obstacles. They also provide a framework for planning your career.

Analyze Your Skills, Reflect on Your Career Decisions

Reflect on the career decisions you've made so far. Why did you make each choice? Did you actually make a choice or just go with the flow somehow? Look for patterns or connective threads. Why? Because it helps to know both how you got where you are and where you are going. There's a book title that stays with me: *If You Don't Know Where You're Going You're Liable to End Up Somewhere Else*. Or, as the Cheshire Cat says, in *Alice in Wonderland*:

> *"Would you tell me, please, which way I ought to go from here?"*
>
> *"That depends a good deal on where you want to get to," said the Cat.*
>
> *"I don't much care where—" said Alice.*
>
> *"Then it doesn't matter which way you go," said the Cat.*
>
> Lewis Carroll

Life History or Skills List

Document every skill and talent you have. You can write a detailed life history that will give you some insight into your development over time, your reaction to unfortunate experiences, and the environments in which you thrived. I constructed a chronological life history for this book, describing in some detail not only every job I've had but also the general environment, grounding the work in time. I thought I'd captured everything and had the experiences in the correct sequence until I unearthed some old resumes and discovered some work experiences I'd totally forgotten. I learned some new things about myself in the process.

Although knowing yourself is more complete if you write your full life history, at a bare minimum you can learn a lot by creating a detailed skills list. Reflect on your life and create a master list of all your skills. This can range from baking great cookies through being the star of your soccer team to advanced computer skills. Make the list as long as you can. Include every experience that added skills – jobs, volunteering, clubs, extracurricular activities, sports, hobbies, and home/family responsibilities. Now, go back and add specific skills for each experience. Don't leave anything out. For example, do you cook? That involves reading, shopping, knowing prices, planning the components of the meal, understanding nutrition, weighing and measuring – at a minimum. Be thorough.

Identify Your Successes

Start reading through your life history. Read slowly and carefully to identify and mark your successes. Mark them all. Add additional successes that occur to you as you do this.

Until you see it written down, you may have no idea of all the things that you have done well, all the obstacles you have overcome, all the people you have influenced. Now is the time for you – finally – to be impressed with yourself.

As you read each incident that makes up your life history, concentrate on the evidence of success. If, as you read, you realize that you have glossed over an event, write more. Once you've identified your successes, you'll be looking at how you felt at the time.

Feelings About Success

Review each success to identify the emotions related to the experience to link your feelings to your achievements. While usually success makes us feel good about ourselves and about the world, sometimes success leaves us feeling vulnerable – either that we're in over our heads and will be found out to be a fraud or that something horrible will happen and our success will collapse.

Now, go back over every success that you marked and answer the following questions:

How was I feeling about myself at the beginning of this experience?

Your purpose here is to learn from your successes so that you can repeat them. Your emotional state, whether you realize it or not, had some influence on the actions you took.

Emotions can't be separated from action. Intuitively, we understand the importance of context and of emotions in understanding our actions.

If you have lost touch with your emotional context, this is a good time to begin flexing those intuitive muscles. Reclaim your emotions and understand exactly how they work for you. This is a big part of owning – being fully in touch with – all aspects of your own life. Recognize that no one ever operates in a vacuum. You are part of a universe rich in hopes, dreams, fantasies, and feelings as well as actions. Which of these have guided you to make the right choice?

If I was experiencing negative emotions, what did I do to use them in a positive way OR what did I do to work through them or get beyond them?

Were you afraid? What did that feel like? How clearly can you identify your fear? In what ways did being afraid stop or limit your actions? Did you make choices based on what was safest? Were you unable to make a choice? How long did that last? If you worked through your fear, how were you able to do this? Did you develop a technique that you were able to transfer to other situations?

If I was experiencing a positive emotion, what was it? How did I use it?

What did success feel like? How do you use those feelings as motivation in other situations?

Past Influences

Review each success to identify how you achieved your successes.

How did I plan for this? What in my life prepared me for this experience?

Even the most serendipitous events in our lives can reveal some prior preparation. Connecting to the skills and experiences that have prepared you for a challenge helps you become clearer about what is at your disposal as you move to new challenges in the future. Marcia Sinetar, author of *To Build the Life You Want, Create the Work You Love,* identified a group she calls Creative Adapters; people who "don't simply adjust, they improvise with superior figuring-out skills." You are identifying your own skills in creative adaptation in this exercise.

What did I do well?

Sometimes, you are the last person to recognize your own strengths. This phenomenon is something we have often seen when working with organizations. People in organizations make extraordinary things happen every day but are often oblivious to their own success. "We got lucky," they say. "Somehow it just worked out." Don't believe this for a second! If you talk to these people long enough about how it "just happened," you can begin to tease out the thought, the skills, the prior practice that led to the right decisions at the right time.

You need to be able to do the analysis that tells you exactly why you succeeded every bit as much as organizations do. The problem in the workplace is that if the individuals who make up an organization are going to learn and grow – and repeat their successes – they have to understand what they did right. So do you. You have to understand the pattern of your successes. You need to know what you drew on from your prior experience at this moment so that next time you are faced with a challenge you can do the same thing. How can you repeat a positive behavior if you don't know what it is?

What events in my past helped me understand this situation? What skills did I develop in other areas that I was able to transfer to this situation?

Have you developed skills that you were able to rely on because you had this experience before, or did you generalize and transfer skills from other – seemingly unrelated – experiences? Are there events in your past that made you avoid certain options or choices? Did your past experience serve you well or did it prevent you from selecting the best plan of action as quickly as you might have wanted?

Identify Challenges

Identify all the rough spots in your life to learn how you have handled challenges.

How was I feeling about this experience?

Some people see hardships or problems as challenges or opportunities. Others see them as insurmountable obstacles.

What was I imagining could happen? Were my worst fears realized?

There are two reasons for writing down your worst fears. One is that sometimes just seeing them in writing restores a sense of perspective. The second reason is that, for many people, this is a crucial step in remembering what planning was done to meet the challenge.

It may be that at the time you actually did engage in a little catastrophizing. Where did that lead? Were you paralyzed or did you move on? Sometimes, dealing with worst-case scenarios helps spur creativity and leads to new – unexpected – courses of action.

How was I feeling about myself during this experience? Did I feel in control or out of control?

We spoke earlier about identifying emotions. Sense of control is related to but may be slightly different than fear and anxiety, so it is important to look at it separately. We see this same theme of letting go of control in Buddhism, in Gestalt therapy, and in existentialism – the notion of living in the moment. How often have you done this? How comfortable were you?

What did I do to resolve the situation? What did I do for myself to cope?

Everyone reacts differently in what they perceive to be a crisis. Some have spent so much time creating contingency plans for every imaginable situation in life that they need only select the appropriate one and proceed. Others take the ostrich route, hide, do nothing, and wait for the crisis to blow over. A third group, true pessimists or fatalists (or both) to the end, simply remain passive, neither hiding nor taking action. They predict that the outcome will be bad and feel that nothing can be done to change it. They wait until the crisis has passed, shrug, and pick up the pieces – if there are any – and start over.

Then there are those whose lives seem to be one big crisis. This group is the perpetually problem-laden. Their lives never run smoothly, but they never see any of their problems as of their own making. They do have one special talent, however; they can always find someone to sort things out for them. People flock to these people's sides to solve their problems. Of course, these people also have a gift for making their helpers feel genuinely appreciative. They are grateful for all assistance and often reciprocate in every way that they can.

A second group mirrors the fatalists discussed earlier. They know that their lives will be a series of chaotic situations. They are not by nature planners, nor are they pessimists. They ride out every crisis, usually taking random actions without evaluating the impact of these actions. Sometimes everything works out wonderfully well; sometimes it's a bust. These people rarely know why.

A third group thrives on chaos. They expect that all change requires a certain amount of confusion and feel that life is a nugget of gold, shaped by fire and blows into something beautiful. Their confidence helps them get through crises.

Which type are you? Are you a whole other type? Does your crisis mode move you forward or hold you back?

Who helped me? How? Did I ask for help or was it offered?

We rarely succeed in a vacuum, but we sometimes do not understand our own pattern for seeking help. Some acknowledge the support of their friends at every turn; others may not realize just how much support they have had. This is a good place to do a quick inventory. You will be looking at two things at once.

First, you will be creating a list of your supporters. This list will be organized into categories elsewhere, but as you create the list, you should begin to look for patterns. Do you rely on a wide circle of supporters or just a few? Do you rely on certain people for only one kind of help? Second, try to remember how you felt about actually asking for help.

Influences on Your Life

Review each success to identify the people who helped you along the way to remind yourself of who your friends are.

Who influenced you? Who have you influenced? Who are all the people you have touched in your life? How did you influence them?

We often think that we go through life unnoticed. We think that we have not contributed anything to the greater good. It is easy to fall into a depression and feel useless. This exercise will remind you of just how much of an influence you are. Make the list as long as you can.

As we move through our own life, we touch so many others' lives, yet we rarely are aware of the impact we have on others. Use your life history as a resource for this list. Work with two columns here so that, as names occur to you (or descriptions if the names are gone), you can add them to either side. Some names may belong on both sides of the list.

Reflect on Your Career Decisions

Reflect on the career decisions you've made so far. Why did you make each choice? Did you actually make a choice or just go with the flow somehow? Look for patterns or connective threads. Why? Because it helps to know both how you got where you are and where you are going.

Skills Analysis

After you have listed all of your skills in these areas, go back and assign weights to each skill in terms of level of use, level of ability, and level of enjoyment.

How high is your level of ability?

> 5 – I'm great at this
> 4 – I'm better than most
> 3 – I'm just about average
> 2 – This is really not one of my best things
> 1 – Are you sure you want to let me touch this?

How often do you use this skill?

> 5 – About as often as I breathe
> 4 – Most of my time centers around this
> 3 – Maybe half the time or a little less
> 2 – Often enough to remember how to use it
> 1 – What skill was that?

How much do you enjoy using this skill?

> 5 – I would probably pay to be able to do this
> 4 – Few things in life make me happier
> 3 – Take it or leave it
> 2 – Maybe someone else would like to give it a try?
> 1 –It sets my teeth on edge

Here's an example of weighted skills:

Skill	Level	Use	Enjoy
podcasting	4	2	4
creating new programs	3	4	2
presentation skills	5	1	5
develop mentoring programs	3	3	2

Create a second list that contains all your potential challenges. This will help you develop a skills grid.

Skills Categories

When you have finished, you will be able to divide your skills into four categories:

> Display shelf – skills to be used most
> Building blocks – skills or behaviors that can be developed
> Recycle – skills or behaviors that can be used differently
> Goodwill/trash heap – skills or behaviors that we want to throw away

Display shelf	Building Blocks
Recycle	Trash Heap

List four to six skills in each category.

Update this grid on a regular basis – at least annually. When you're ready to explore new possibilities, look for jobs or experiences that rely on your display shelf skills, supported by building block skills. Avoid Recycle and Trash Heap skills. Evaluate what's in each quadrant in terms of your list of challenges. Decide what, if any, trade-offs you are willing to make.

Summary of my skills and challenges through college:

Skills and Assets	Potential Obstacles
Solid Foundation	Learned to stay in the background
Resilience	Loss of trust
Working with children	Low self-esteem
Creativity	Poor self-image
Writing	Needing external validation
Typing and filing	Poor typing skills
Wardrobe planning/coordination	Weight issues
Public speaking ability	Hate public speaking

Each time you are evaluating a career choice, review these two charts. One of the best pieces of career advice I ever got was that it is just as important to know what you don't want as it is to know what you want. What are you passionate about? Are you willing to deal with an obstacle to do what you love?

For example, I'm willing to deal with public speaking because I love to teach and do workshops. I'm willing to type in order to write books or create curriculum yet will never again type as a core job responsibility. Know your trade-offs. Know how and when you are willing to use your non-preferred (recycle) skills (and for how long) in order to make a dream come true. Review your trade-offs periodically.

Know Your Values

There are three areas to look at as you think about potential career choices. We've talked about identifying potential challenges and organizing your skills. Another filter that will improve the quality of your choices is understanding your values. After all, your values define who you are. They also inform every choice you make – especially your career choices. Not only are you looking for work that reflects your core values but also work that does not honor those values.

You might not choose a position that required such long work hours that you could no longer spend time with your children or participate in meetings or leisure activities. If animal rights are high on your values list it would not be easy for you to work for an organization that experiments on animals. The interplay of these three factors will enhance your exploration and your choices.

Values List

Select your top 10–15 values. Use this list as a start and add others as you wish.

Achievement	Helping others	Purity
Advancement	Honesty	Quality of endeavors
Adventure	Independence	Quality of relationships
Affection	Influence	Recognition
Arts	Inner harmony	Religion
Challenging problems	Integrity	Responsibility/ accountability
Change/variety	Intellectual status	Safety
Community	Job tranquility	Security
Competence	Joy	Self-respect
Cooperation	Knowledge	Serenity
Country	Leadership	Sophistication
Creativity	Location	Stability
Decisiveness	Loyalty	Supervising others
Democracy	Market position	Time freedom
Ecological awareness	Meaningful work	Truth
Economic security	Merit	Wealth
Effectiveness	Money	Wisdom
Ethical practice	Nature	Work under pressure
Excellence	Order/calm/conformity	Work with others
Excitement	Peace	Working alone
Expertise	Personal growth	
Fame	Physical challenge	
Family	Pleasure	
Fast-paced work	Power/Authority	
Financial gain	Privacy	
Freedom	Professionalism	
Fullest life/up to potential	Public service	

How will your core values influence your career choices?

Dr. Susan R. Meyer

Writing Your Eulogy

One way to begin to see what's important in your life is to look ahead to the end of your years. To do this, you are about to write your own eulogy. This may sound morbid, but it really isn't. The purpose of this exercise is to craft a personal vision.

Organizations do this all the time. They hire expensive consultants to lead them in future searches or "blue skying" because they know that they can't grow or change unless they know where they want to be – the organizational vision. Just as for organizations, when you as an individual understand that vision – what you hope to achieve during the course of your life – your life goals will become clear to you.

Imagine that you are writing your own eulogy. If you find the idea of writing a eulogy upsetting or threatening, picture yourself writing a testimonial being given about you at a big awards banquet honoring your lifetime achievements. Find a quiet, private space and something to write on. Turn off the television. Get rid of any distractions. Take a few deep breaths. Clear your mind of other concerns. If you wish, close your eyes.

Imagine a room full of people who love you who have come together to celebrate your life. Imagine that you have accomplished everything that you ever hoped to do. Your every dream has been fulfilled. Everyone who is important to you is gathered to talk about the wonderful person you were and about your many accomplishments. If you listen, you can hear the speakers. Write down what they are saying about you.

What are all the things you have accomplished? Have you traveled? Where? What have you created? Have you written or painted or played the flute or knitted or gardened? Did you cook for friends? Volunteer at a soup kitchen? Teach someone something? Send perfect postcards or birthday cards?

Write as quickly as you can and don't censor your writing. When you have written as much as you can, put it aside overnight. Now go back to your eulogy and read it very slowly. What did you leave out? Make any additions you feel are important.

Vision Statement

Your personal vision statement should describe what you ultimately envision the greater purpose of your life to be, in terms of growth, values, contributions to society, etc. As you grow and change, your vision and mission may also change. Self-reflection is a vital activity if you want to develop a meaningful vision.

Once you have defined your vision, you can begin to develop strategies for moving toward that vision. Part of this includes the development of a mission statement. What do you want for the rest of your life? Take a few minutes to write down your personal vision. This will be based on your goals and values.

Mission Statement

Vision statements and mission statements are very different. Your mission statement is the vision translated into written form. It is a concrete expression of how you will bring your vision to life. A mission statement should be a short and concise statement of goals and priorities.

Your mission statement should be a concise statement of strategy, and it should fit with your vision. The mission should answer three questions:

What will I do?

How will I do it?

For whom will I do it?

What will I do? This question should be answered in terms of what are the concrete and psychological needs that you want to fulfill.

How will I do it? This question captures the more technical elements.

For whom will I do it? The answer to this question is also vital, as it will help you focus your efforts.

Goals

What do you now see as the overall goal of your life? This is generally called an overarching goal. Think of this overarching goal as your mental picture of your career/life trajectory. It's helpful to review your goals periodically to eliminate those that are either completed or no longer relevant and to add new ones.

Write down the biggest current goal you can think of – a real stretch goal – something that will definitely expand your comfort zone. This is your overarching goal, not dissimilar from your personal mission statement, simply a bit more refined – more specific. Then, you will become even more specific as you plan out your sub-goals that support the overarching goal.

Perhaps the simplest way to bring your goal from general to specific is to use a proven goal-setting formula: S-M-A-R-T goals. Check your goal against the S-M-A-R-T criteria and tweak away until it's as clear and strong as possible. When you design a home, if you don't have a really good sense of what the completed building looks like, it will be hard to plan the individual rooms. The criteria are described below.

Specific – as detailed as possible

Measurable – criteria that will indicate progress toward and completion of the goal

Achievable – Is this something that you can actually do?

Realistic – Can this actually happen?

Timely/Time-framed – How long will this take? Is this the right goal for right now?

Chapter 3

Stuck Spots – Exploration, New Possibilities, and Support

It's likely that there will be times in your career when you may just feel stuck. There will be times when life or world events upend your life in unexpected ways. Your needs may change. You may find that you need less or more money to support your lifestyle. You may find that your current career has too many or too few physical demands.

The job market changes. Some careers simply cease to exist. At one point, as computer applications grew at a tremendous rate, there was an enormous need for users' manuals and therefore for technical writers. Demand exceeded supply. A decade or so later, the market suddenly dried up, perhaps as these jobs, like many customer service operations, were outsourced overseas. At the same time, entrepreneurial opportunities continue to grow.

Our lives change. Family needs may require fewer work hours. Health concerns may dictate relocation. You may need flexible hours or a different shift to accommodate child or elder care.

The world changes. After the destruction of the World Trade Center, many were reluctant to return to the area. Some never worked there again. The Covid-19 pandemic caused many people to think about their mortality and how they wanted to spend the rest of their lives. Some refused to continue in low-pay, high-risk positions unless conditions changed. Others simply quit. Some refused to return to traditional workplaces, preferring remote work.

You know your skills, values assets, and liabilities. You may have tried a few career directions or simply haven't figured out your trajectory and have drifted for a while, taking whatever comes your way, perhaps out of necessity. At times like this, there are two important focus areas: being sure that your support network is strong – perhaps even adding a few more people – and being open to all possibilities. When you widen your focus and don't rule any possibility out, you will be surprised at the new things that will appear.

Talk to everyone. Often, someone knows someone who knows someone. That's exactly how I discovered early childhood education. A girlfriend's boyfriend was a substitute teacher in a day care center. They needed another sub and he suggested me. Then, someone at that center heard about a permanent opening at another center. That same grapevine led to a move to a higher-level position at another center.

Fantasize. Make lists of everything you might want to do and go back to your skills list to see how your skills might fit each. Remember the woman whose list of possibilities included circus clown? She needed that crazy idea as a jumping off point to get to her career in politics. Problem-solving theory calls this breaking set. A ridiculous suggestion opens your brain up to a whole new group of ideas.

When everything seems to come to a screeching halt, you'll need to stop, take a deep breath, and regroup. Reframe this as a challenge and a potential step forward. This is where the goal-planning tools in the last chapter will help you reset your course.

After I finished my master's in Educational Psychology/Reading, I once again didn't know what I was going to do for a living. I managed to get a temporary job with a reading program that was being introduced into elementary school. That lasted twelve weeks. Then I had the opportunity to sub in a day care center. I enjoyed the work and eventually found an assistant teacher's position in Greenwich Village. My colleagues as well as the parents were almost all hippies. It was a very mellow existence with children named Apache and Moonbeam and mothers who designed tie-dyed shirts or clothing made from dishcloths. I enjoyed working with young children, loved the minimal structure, and this fit my lifestyle perfectly. For a while, I was very happy not being in charge of anything.

I had moved on to become a head teacher at another day care center by this time and had also moved out of Manhattan to an apartment just off the King's Highway train station in Brooklyn. I was warned that this was a bad move and that spending all my time with my close friend and her family would make me pretty much a social isolate. I did it anyway and found that my social life evaporated. This repeats the old introvert-social butterfly dichotomy from my childhood.

The new center had an emphasis on mental health, and I became increasingly involved with children with emotional problems. I also started a reading readiness program. With an Iranian assistant and a Cuban aide, I had an international team supplemented by volunteers and mental health workers. I enjoyed my day care experience, and it gave me the opportunity to nurture many children who needed me. At the same time, I took an active role in parenting my goddaughter. These activities allowed me to fulfill my maternal needs.

Eventually, though, I became much more interested in the needs of the parents. I managed to have my staff working so efficiently that I could spend most of my time out in the hall with parents, but I was growing out of the job.

I knew that I didn't want to stay in day care, and I knew that I wanted to do something that involved teaching and counseling adults, but I didn't know exactly what that would look like, so I did something I was very good at – I went back to school. Unfortunately, I didn't think much about how I was going to pay the bills. I was able to eke out an existence for a while with a student loan and unemployment.

I had gone back for my second master's, in Counseling, without a plan. I don't think I had even heard of mission, vision, and goals at this point.

While I was trying to figure things out, I reconsidered teaching and subbed for a few days in the public schools. This generally meant keeping the class from running wild or leaving the room before the end of the period. I accepted an assignment in a vocational high school and was actually given a lesson plan and was expected to teach a class of what appeared to be plumbing majors, judging from the bags of pipe they had under their desks. I couldn't even get started. They started insulting me from head to toe and all I could do was clench my fists and keep thinking, *I will not cry. I will not cry.* Eventually, a vice principal and a security guard came in. The vice principal put me in an office for the rest of the day. This reinforced what I felt about my classroom management skills when I had finished my student teaching. I hated it so much that I took my phone off the hook every morning for the rest of the year.

About this time, a good friend in my second master's program – this time in counseling – invited me to join him at a taping of $20,000 Pyramid. He had always wanted to be a contestant. I'd never really thought about it, but it sounded like an interesting way to spend the day. I was invited to try out to become a contestant, and just at the point where I was considering bankruptcy as an option, I was selected for the show.

Now, if that master's program had prepared me for anything, it had prepared me for television. It felt like every class we took was taped. I had no fear of being on camera. Four years as an English major in college plus high school Latin, German, and Greek made me good with words.

Moving a number of times helped too. The clue "things that you crack" was one I'd learned in Pennsylvania and led to the response "a window" for the big win. I had the skills for this. Twenty-nine seconds after the game began, I was $10,000 richer. That money got me through the next year.

By this time, I recognized a pattern in my life – I was the queen of the eleventh-hour comeback. I had learned to rely on myself by the time I was nine. By the time I was in my mid-twenties, I had broadened that out to trust in the universe. No matter how bad things got, if I kept my mind open, did everything I could think of to do to aid the process, and believed that everything would be okay, everything always was.

Of course, I also found out quickly that meditation and reliance on the universe was not going to be enough if I didn't do my part. I have a vivid memory of deciding to repaint my kitchen while preparing dinner for friends. I was calm and serene – I could get everything done. The universe would provide. Well, neither one of us turned on the oven, so my guests, faced with a raw chicken, had a vegetarian evening!

The moral of this story is God helps those who help themselves. Setting intentions and visualizing are wonderfully supportive techniques. They help you have a clear picture of what you want to be. But there's always an action component. Take a baby step if you're not clear on the big steps.

I also began to learn that how you view yourself in terms of success and failure can only come from within yourself. The problem, of course, is that we tend to measure ourselves by our peers. And sometimes, we have a real overachieving group of peers. One of my fellow interns at the counseling center was a wonderful woman with excellent counseling skills. Her only problem was that she saw herself as a nobody. She never felt that she was as good as her husband and friends.

This was a hard one. Her husband had been part of a former president's cabinet. Her two closest women friends were successful professionals. One of them, Barbara Howar, had just signed the biggest book deal on record. The other was the internationally known media figure Barbara Walters. Tough competition! It took a lot of work to help my friend recognize that she had chosen a different – lower-profile – field and was brilliant at what she did and every bit as successful in her own right.

This is something I'm still working on today. I still don't always recognize my own successes. As a counseling intern I had helped establish the new counseling center. I enjoyed the process of getting something new going. It drew on the same skills that I had used to successfully transform my preschool classroom.

There were four part-time counselors on staff. As interns, we met weekly with our advisor to discuss our progress and to discuss the interactions among the group members. At the last session, we were all asked to talk about the things that we felt were important – had gone well. I spoke about the camaraderie among the group and how pleased I was that we could all confide in each other and were supportive of each other. I was shocked when one of my peers said, "But Susan, we all come to YOU!" It was like getting a standing ovation. It's a good example of my lack of recognition of my own strengths.

This goes back to something that coach and author (including A Return to Love) Marianne Williamson stresses. We all need to acknowledge our strengths and successes. Donna Steinhorn, one of my coaches, had me make lists of my successes (with proof) and lists of all the people who liked me (also with evidence) and keep them in my office area to review when I was feeling worthless. I've done this with many of my clients as well.

Make your lists. Review them regularly and add to them. We all have those days where we find ourselves singing the old camp ditty, "Nobody loves me, everybody hates me, think I'm gonna eat some worms." Don't do it – remember that lots of people love you and skip the upset stomach. Read your list! Read it several times a day if you need to. You're pretty special, aren't you?

Knowing your skills and potential gaps is essential for the serial careerist. Eventually, I came to the realization that years of working in day care would not make potential employers automatically assume that I would be good with adults.

I registered with employment agencies and got sent out on temp jobs that depended on my woeful clerical skills. Finally, I was sent to an employment agency to interview for a receptionist position. During the interview they decided that I was better suited to being assistant to the comptroller and I found myself in charge of the temp payroll. This was a nightmare – remember my math phobia? Every week I was sure that I'd make a huge mistake and that a mob of angry temps would come after me because they didn't get their checks. I couldn't take the pressure and finally quit, believing that I was about to be offered a counseling position at a SUNY college.

Unfortunately, there was no reality to that dream, and I ended up working for another agency, this time soliciting openings and making placements. I hated it. I was no good at selling. I hated the impossibility of placing clients who didn't have the "corporate crisp" look that was expected. I hated that the other placement counselors would make fun of applicants who didn't live up to their standards of appearance. Although I was excellent with the applicants (using my career counseling skills), I rarely got job listings.

This was a base salary plus commission job. Because I wasn't making placements, I wasn't getting commission checks. The base salary was $150 a week, just about enough to barely cover my expenses. The wardrobe coordination skills that I'd developed in high school enabled me to dress appropriately on a very limited budget. The cooking skills that were pretty much in my blood enabled me to stretch a pound of spaghetti with homemade meat sauce (ground beef was still cheap) into a week's worth of dinners when I was really broke. My colleagues weren't doing that much better. For the price of a Happy Hour drink, we loaded up on free bar food for dinner as often as possible.

In the meantime, I was building credibility as someone who worked with adults. After a few months, a woman who was to become a close friend joined the staff. She immediately began badgering me to leave, telling me repeatedly that I was in the wrong field and encouraging me to resume my job search. I'm eternally grateful to her.

Exactly one year after I had taken my first employment agency job, I found a position as a cooperative education coordinator within the City University of New York. They needed someone with counseling skills and a knowledge of the secretarial field. A year of placing office personnel plus my master's degree made me the perfect candidate.

I spent seven years working in the Cooperative Education Program at Medgar Evers, a primarily Black CUNY college. When I started, the average student age was twenty-six and the population was over-whelmingly female. I loved the students. It was a little strange being a minority faculty member – one of a handful of whites. It was also difficult at times to find a niche at the college as someone perceived as an administrator in a sea of academics and as a grant-funded employ-ee rather than on a college line. These distinctions brought out other biases and issues around status. My own experiences at the college made it easier for me to help my students learn to succeed in work en-vironments where race, age, education, and status were often issues.

At the college, I developed a career planning course that focused on life histories and discovered many unforgettable women. I had de-veloped an interest in women's life histories when I was getting my master's in Counseling. While working at the college, I became in-creasingly fascinated with life histories. I also decided that, if I was going to establish myself in academia, I needed my doctorate. I knew that I would never return to NYU, so I investigated Teachers College, Columbia.

I discovered that there was a field of study called Adult and Continuing Education. I really knew nothing about the field of adult education, but I reasoned that at least the population would always be around. As I looked at the program more closely, I realized that it was the per-fect field to bring together my interests in counseling and teaching.

Counseling had fulfilled my need to help people. My interest in the field, however, was focused on practical concerns. I was most interested in how counseling could be used as a teaching tool. It was in co-op that I was finally able to blend all my skills – teaching, counseling, job placement. Because the population at Medgar Evers was primarily women, primarily Black and primarily older than the general college population, working there had deepened my interest in researching what drove my students and how I could best help them move into a meaningful career.

I never regretted a minute of my doctoral program. The classes were so different from anything I'd ever experienced! I thought I'd died and gone to academic heaven. My first course was Adult Development and our first assignment was to write a life history. And fit it into two pages. The interview was easy; editing it down took hours. I knew that I needed to do more, and the germ of my dissertation sprouted in that class.

I've always felt a strong pull between theory and practice and have spent most of my career trying to successfully integrate the two. Although I enjoy a good theory and really like synthesizing diverse information to generate theories of my own, I have no patience for something that can't be put into – or at least connected to – practice. I needed to find settings where I could use my theoretical background to make something happen.

I became involved in planning a conference on transformative learning and be a small part of working to develop a theory of transformative learning. It also provided me the opportunity to become part of the adjunct faculty and later to advise doctoral candidates. This also led to being asked to organize the Workplace Learning Institute, an event that brought together cutting-edge theorists, well-known practitioners, faculty, and graduate students.

I was working very hard, juggling a full-time job and full-time graduate study. I didn't have any time left for more of a social life than a quick coffee before class. As the pressure to finish my dissertation before my fortieth birthday and before grant funding for the co-op program ran out, I was barely speaking to even my closest friends. David's Cookies was my new best friend! (A chocolate chip cookie and a little television were my rewards for completing segments of the dissertation.)

Unfortunately, I had lost my entire circle of non-edible, non-grad student friends through neglect. It took me years to rebuild my circle. The habit of isolation required to speed through the degree and the dissertation, underscored by my natural introverted tendencies that grew out of the need to stay invisible as a child and adolescent, made it harder to develop new friendships.

If you were a Brownie Scout, you may remember singing, "Make new friends but keep the old. One is silver and the other is gold." Good advice. Take time for yourself no matter how involved you are in a project. Go out with your friends or family once a week. Cherish your inner circle. Your outer circle will expand and contract depending on circumstances. Mothers often find that few of the relationships they formed because of their children last. Those drinking buddies from your last job can fade away pretty quickly. Marriage counselors often advise couples to have date nights. Use that advice to ensure that you always have a circle that supports you and that you support.

Expanded Skills, Assets, and Potential Obstacles Chart

Skills and Assets	Potential Obstacles
Solid Foundation	Learned to stay in the background
Resilience	Loss of trust
Working with children	Low self
Creativity	Poor self
Writing	Needing external validation

Typing and filing	Poor typing skills
Wardrobe planning/ coordination	Weight issues
Public speaking ability	Hate public speaking

What's important for you in this part of my story?

Knowing and reviewing your skill set will make it easier to understand what you'll need for a transition and how to address any deficits. I knew that I had the skills to work with adults but lacked credibility, so I took time to address that. I didn't realize that my wardrobe planning and cooking skills were going to be essential to my survival. Don't overlook any of your skills. They may be essential to transitions.

Come as close as you can to maintaining a balance in your life by taking time for fun and by maintaining connections to your friends and family. Making time for socializing and relaxing will actually increase your productivity (and maintain your sanity).

For the curious and restless group: Research on adult development indicates that our twenties and thirties are a period of exploration. For some, this is a lifelong pattern. What becomes important is having an overall vision that's consistent with your core values. This tells you what kind of life you want to live. Exploration and openness are the tools that give you the widest latitude in your exploration and keep you from drifting aimlessly.

For the mid- to late-career group: This is a good point to reassess your mission, vision, and goals. At midlife, there's usually a shift from achievement to meaning making. This is a good time to be sure that you are on your true path. As Thomas Merton, Trappist monk and author of *The Seven Storey Mountain*, said, "People may spend their whole lives climbing the ladder of success only to find, once they reach the top, that the ladder is leaning against the wrong wall." What has changed in your life that might suggest moving your ladder?

For the late entry or re-entry group: Reassess your life experiences. Mine for hidden skills and abilities. Look at talents that you've never explored or that may have seemed irrelevant until now.

The exercises in this chapter are designed to help you maintain balance and perspective and to open up new possibilities.

Strategy 3: Maintain and Expand Relationships

Exercises

Who's in your support network?

Create and maintain your support circle. This is a four-square model. Put two different names in each box. You'll want to do this so you aren't over-relying on one person. Also, the names in each box should be different so that you are not asking the same person to play too many roles. The chart looks like this:

Cheerleaders	Comforters
Critics	Confronters

Everyone needs *cheerleaders*. These are the people who applaud you for getting your shoes on the right feet. They provide unconditional support for everything that you do. They make you feel brilliant and invincible. You need them for those days when you're convinced that you are useless, talentless, and totally incapable.

Comforters provide totally non-judgmental support. They will listen for hours and agree with everything you say. They show up with wine and chocolate and a full box of tissues. They bundle you up in a quilt and listen and listen and listen. They stay until they know you are soothed.

Critics help you think things through and find potential flaws in your plans. They do this in a loving way, helping you to find better solutions or create foolproof plans or take your writing from so-so to outstanding.

Confronters call you on your crap. They ask you what you've done about the things you've said you'd do. They are the ones who ensure that you don't hide behind excuses and actually get things done.

These are the people who help you get through life. They're the ones who help you make hard decisions and recover from disasters and take care of yourself and rise to greatness. You'll want a second chart, by the way, that shows you who you support. Refresh your charts twice a year to be sure that the people you have in place are still part of your life in the same way.

Your support network will be right there to help you if life becomes too overwhelming and you need more help than they can give. They'll help you research your options, evaluate your choices, and make sure that you show up for your appointments.

Vision Meditation

Take five minutes each day to envision the life you want for yourself. Create, in your mind, a detailed picture of how you are living this ideal life. Be very specific. See yourself in that life. Don't think about how you'll achieve this; focus on what it looks like, feels like. Getting caught up in the "hows" limits you. Seeing the big picture opens up possibilities and creates opportunities for synchronicity.

Widen Your Vision of What's Out There

If you keep your eyes open to what you're looking for it will appear. Maybe not quite as you'd envisioned it, but it will be there. An old exercise suggests looking for a red car. Once you see the first one, they will be popping up all over the place. This applies to opportunities as well. If I hadn't followed up on an invitation to a taping of *Pyramid*, I would never have won enough money to live on for a year.

Chapter 4

Trying a Stable Job with a Good Pension

There may come a time when the serial careerist wants or needs a more stable work life. That may mean staying in one job for a longer period of time or may mean moving through a series of related positions. For me, that meant settling into civil service for a long period of time, moving through several positions in municipal government. Each position brought different challenges; each was a very different environment, so each felt very much like a career change. Each position involved recombining my core skills and applying what I knew in a variety of different ways.

In every job I have had, I have worked to improve things. I'm driven to be successful at whatever I do, and to be perceived as knowledgeable and a leader, although I don't necessarily want this for the power – more for the recognition and for people coming to me for assistance.

Counseling had fulfilled my need to help people. My interest in the field, however, was limited to practical concerns. I was most interested in how counseling could be used as a teaching tool. It was as a Cooperative Education coordinator at Medgar Evers, a CUNY College, that I was finally able to blend all my skills – teaching, counseling, and job placement. I became totally immersed in my work. I revised the curriculum for the four Co-op placement courses and became involved in the departmental curriculum committee, established to set up a uniform career development curriculum across programs. I established a career library. I designed a workshop to train faculty coordinators.

When the federal grant money for the Co-op program finally ran out, I had to leave the college. I tried to make the transition to independent consultant but didn't have the marketing skills or confidence to get clients. I looked for another college counseling position but was unwilling to leave New York because I didn't want to leave my family and friends. Finally, when I was running out of money and ideas, I remembered that a former student of mine, who worked in the Mayor's Office, had told me to give him a call if I was ever looking for work. This was several years later, but I needed another eleventh-hour miracle, so I called him. Within days I had a new job at the Human Resources Administration's Office (HRA) of Staff Development and Training (OSDT) at a considerably higher salary, benefits, and a pension.

At HRA, I had to hit the ground running. I had a brand new doctorate in Adult Education, but no idea what HRA was about and, other than the one workshop, no experience with staff development. At least my teaching in the Co-op program was very similar to training, so I had transferable skills to draw on. Also, I was lucky to be working with two managers who were generous teachers.

I was immediately immersed in AIDS Awareness training. This was an entirely new field and called on everything I'd learned in every psychology and transformative learning course and all my coaching skills as we wrestled with developing programs that were both informational – there was a lot of false information about transmission – and attitudinal. AIDS was just coming to the forefront as an issue for welfare clients. It was taking a toll on people who might be classified as traditional welfare recipients – IV drug users, etc.

AIDS also created a whole new group requiring services. Many new applicants were middle- to upper-middle-class men. Before they became ill, they had held a much higher standard of living than most recipients. The rents that they could no longer pay were far higher; the medical care they needed was much greater and more expensive. These were also people who were unfamiliar with the Income Maintenance bureaucracy and often too weak to cope with it. There were high levels of fear and resentment among staff assigned to clients with AIDS.

We needed to immediately launch a massive education campaign for personnel who had no information about the disease and little compassion for the clients. I helped develop an executive overview for the commissioner's direct reports. This was the beginning of two years of AIDS Awareness training. I helped develop a train the trainer program and trained 150 trainers in AIDS Awareness. I also designed, supervised, and participated in training for line staff, including all the employees in the City's homeless shelters.

I was not in this job very long before one of the women I reported to left and the other retired. By this time, I was supervising three other trainers, all of whom were social workers with many more years of experience than I had. When my manager retired, I was given most of her responsibilities and now had seven people reporting to me. I continued to be involved in special projects, including designing new caseworker training for the Division of Adult Services.

During this time, I also developed a trainer development program and worked with several hundred trainers to improve their skills. It was through these classes that I was recruited for my next job. One of the women I trained felt that I would be a good person to have at the new Child Welfare academy, a new training unit devoted solely to the preparation of children's protective services workers. I was offered the position of director of Trainer Development.

This was a wonderful opportunity for me to bring together a variety of skills. I was working developmentally with the staff I would be seeing over a long period of time. This meant that I could help each of them add to their skill base at an individualized pace, rather than just a one-shot approach. I was using the curriculum design skills I'd developed at OSDT as well as the adult learning principles from my doctoral studies.

I began to work closely with the curriculum development group as well and had a chance to concentrate more on reflective learning. As we tested out each new curriculum, I worked with the authors to ensure that the material matched the learning intent and that the learner was provided with a developmental path. At the same time, of course, this process further developed the abilities of the trainers and developers. Although I loved my colleagues and the strong sense of dedication and camaraderie that they had with each other, I was, once again, the outsider. I hated the commute, an hour and a half minimum on the subway line known for having the most homeless people sleeping in every car. As the staff became too busy to attend my programs, I grew bored and began seeking new challenges. It was time to move on.

My next move was pure serendipity and again into a totally new area. My former manager at the Academy had accepted a position at NYC's Department of Personnel and had promised to bring me along. She forgot and had interviewed and was about to hire a colleague of mine when her closest friend, at a funeral they were both attending, reminded her that she had planned to hire me. So she did. I accepted a position supervising a Defensive Driving program with the Citywide Department of Personnel. I knew nothing about Defensive Driving, but I wanted the opportunity to supervise staff again. Also, I liked the idea of starting up something new and I was promised the opportunity to expand the job.

What I didn't like was feeling like an outsider – Defensive Driving was regarded as a second-rate program by staff members who worked with the professional development courses. They decided that, despite my record and degrees, I must be second-rate. I felt that I had to prove myself. I became involved in the annual needs assessment and in-program evaluation. This led to setting up an Evaluation Forum and developing Trainer Development courses.

Once again, I'd turned a job in a related organization into a completely different career direction. I quickly started to become involved in the professional development courses. When we decided to implement a new format with certificate programs combining core managerial and supervisory courses and electives, I was part of the development team for the supervisory series and lead for the managerial series. We developed a skills assessment tool that helped participants choose electives to supplement the core training and qualify for a certificate.

I was asked to design a mentoring program for participants in the managerial certificate program. It was another opportunity to use my counseling, adult learning, and transformative learning knowledge. During the next two years, this program grew from fifty participants to 150 and also included managers mentoring supervisors. I had expanded the trainer development series to thirteen courses. I became involved in citywide reengineering projects.

This change became another uphill battle – a theme in my career. Once again, I was the outsider – this time in an organization that believed strongly in promoting people up through the ranks. It took almost four years, but, finally, I was able to carve my own niche as the expert on mentoring and on management development programs.

I was also an adjunct at Teachers College and becoming involved in a new venture there. I was invited to help create the Workplace Learning Institute, a program that would bring students, scholars, and practitioners together to examine issues in the workplace. This was an exciting and productive period where I was able to use all my skills in one position. Unfortunately, the mayor did not see training as all that important. Our programs were about to be cut drastically when my supervisor accepted a new position at MTA NYC Transit Authority and asked me to come along as her deputy.

When I got to the Transit Authority, I found out that they had no intention of making me deputy director and I was going to have to start from the bottom again. I was now training on Substance Abuse Prevention and Diversity, courses designed to meet agency mandates. The environment, overall, was not a good one for women. Track work, bus, and subway maintenance and operation had been traditionally male positions, and although that was beginning to change, change was very slow. Women were sidelined in career growth and sometimes bullied or threatened. One female supervisor told me that, while she was walking a track, a subordinate drove a train right up to her as if he was planning to run her over. When she reported this, she was told that he was "just playing" and that "boys will be boys." So clearly, moving into a more responsible position was going to be an uphill battle.

This attitude carried over to the classroom and trainees were often not willing to listen to female trainers. We developed a proactive opening statement, telling the groups that we knew they probably fell into one of three categories: prisoners, vacationers, and learners. While we hoped that most of them might become learners, our hope was that the prisoners would consider stepping up to vacationers and simply relax and enjoy a quiet day with an actual lunch hour. It generally worked. I also went back to the skills that I'd used in creating skits for my high school variety show to find more interesting and, when possible, humorous ways to deliver the material.

Eventually, some of the departments started asking for specialized programs that basically were emotional intelligence. I had a colleague whom I worked well with and we started developing stress and anger management programs that we disguised as executive communication. I developed a Training Development program for Rapid Transit Operations, which was great fun because I got adopted by all these big training guys who taught people how to operate trains and I had to go out and walk track with them. You haven't lived until you're a short person trying to climb over an electrified rail. Since I was wearing their boss's safety vest, I kept reminding them that he'd be unhappy if his vest got fried.

I was part of a team that created a ten-day leadership development program for supervisors and began team teaching that. We covered everything from regulations through communication to problem-solving. We also began to instill different norms, moving away from command and control to a more person-centered leadership style. The program was very successful and I was asked to lead a team to develop a similar program for managers.

I really did not get along with my boss's boss under any circumstances, and at the same time felt that something odd was going on with me. I was getting really cranky and nasty, and I finally noticed that I couldn't draw a straight line because my hands were shaking so badly. It turned out I had an overactive thyroid. I knew somewhere at the back of my mind this was linked to stress and that was the beginning of the end for me with the Transit Authority because I realized there was a chance this job was going to kill me, so maybe it was time to think about something else to do. But, at the same time, the senior vice president of the Division of Subways came to us with an idea. He said, "I need for my general superintendents to be better problem-solvers and I need them to think on their feet and do good presentations."

I was just burning to do an action learning program. I had fallen in love with the concept and I thought this is what we can do for the general superintendents. We made it a ten-day program, having them come to our office for training segments and then go out in the field, do some observations, and then come back and do some more problem-solving, go back in the field, and come back to brainstorm solutions.

This was not an environment big on learning or researching solutions, or having people who didn't outrank them asking questions, so we got them baseball caps and we made them five-star generals. We got them portfolios so they would look like researchers. When they went out there, they could open up their portfolio and take notes, and when we got to the point where we needed them to sort of start really thinking, we actually said now we want you to all wear your thinking caps and that's when we gave them the baseball caps. They went out there wonderfully empowered and said that they were allowed to ask questions because Joe (the senior vice president) said we could, and they came up with some wonderful ideas.

At the end of the first year, they put together a conference that all of the managers in the Division of Subways were asked to attend. Each group presented the problem they had been working on and the solutions they came up with, and they facilitated small groups in the afternoon to come up with even more suggestions. Most of the ideas were implemented.

We did that for two years. The second year, they opened it up to the supervisors and brought them out for the conference as well, but by that time, I finally realized how much this place was making me crazy. I knew what I liked doing was working with people around problem-solving and around improving their lives. Still, the years I spent in civil service gave me the opportunity to use a number of skills in a variety of combinations.

Here are other examples of recombining skills:

Sarah went to an Ivy League university, planning to get a doctorate in English. The upheavals of the '70s led her to think that the universities might all be closing down when a course got her interested in Medieval history, economics, and politics. She got a tenure track appointment and realized that she wasn't cut out to be a Medieval scholar and wasn't happy with the financial limitations of a professorial career. She passed through advertising, wrote a few science fiction novels, and discovered that her writing and analytic skills were a good match for becoming a certified financial analyst. In time, she decided that those skills were even better suited to marketing and

Dr. Susan R. Meyer

moved into marketing communications, where she interacts with a variety of deliverables including web copy, biographies, white papers, and brochures.

Nancy wanted to be in the fashion industry and was hired by a major department store, but her first boss was a nightmare, so she went on to another department store that had a travel agency and learned to be a travel agent. She planned her honeymoon before moving to another store's fashion office. There, she learned the relationship between looks, feelings about appearance, and self-esteem. That was the seed of a coaching career. The Junior League added training and leadership skills. Eventually, she hired a coach, took coach training, and helped organize a new coaching school, where she co-created programs and trained coaches. That drew on all the skills she had developed except the travel agency skills. Eventually, she co-founded a conference for coaches, again using all of her skills, and became coordinator for an international association of leaders in coaching and personal development, now folding the travel agent skills into the coaching, organizing, and leadership mix.

What's important for you in this section of my story?

Most people who are serial careerists are restless, curious, and sometimes easily bored. If any of these terms apply to you, there's more than one way to satisfy your need for new challenges. I was content to stay within organizations within municipal government because I found new challenges that allowed me to continue to learn and grow. Each position was different enough from the last that I experienced it as a new career. If this is a possibility, you will feel like you've embarked on a new career with each new challenge. With a little creativity and a lot of persistence you can recreate your career many times over without ever changing employers.

If you are now newly embarking on a career outside of home and family responsibilities or returning after an absence, you can translate many of the skills you may not realize that you have into workplace skills. Managing the household expenses is, after all, using the same skills as managing a departmental budget. One of my favorite comparisons came from a female CEO who said that if you could decide who got the last gumdrop, the three-year-old or the five-year-old, you could handle any labor negotiation.

For the curious and restless group: It's possible to have a new career without leaving an organization. View each position as a means to an end – expanding your skill set and allowing you to continue to experiment. One woman moved through three distinctly different areas in a brokerage over a decade before discovering the perfect position in writing in the marketing department.

For the mid- to late-career group: Perhaps this is a decision point. For some, this is a point to think about legacy. What do you have to teach others? Who can you mentor? Are there other career options that you'd like to explore?

For the late entry or re-entry group: How can you view your life experiences as a career path? As you review your skills, you have two tasks: be sure that you've included everything and group your skills, as far as possible, into a developmental sequence.

Strategy 4: Recombine Skills

Exercises

Update Your Skills List

Example: My Expanded Skills, Assets, and Potential Obstacles Chart

(Note that some obstacles have been eliminated or have become irrelevant. Since the advent of keyboarding and computerized files, speed, accuracy, and duplicating don't have the same relevance, for example.)

Skills and Assets	Potential Obstacles
Solid Foundation	~~Learned to stay in the background~~
Resilience	Loss of trust

Working with children	Low self-esteem
Creativity	Poor self-image
Writing	Needing external validation
Typing and filing	Poor typing skills
Wardrobe planning/coordination	Weight issues
Public speaking ability	Hate public speaking
Curriculum development	
Career coaching	
Conference planning	
Leadership	
Coordination	
Writing	

What skills have you learned since you made your original list?

Are there skills that need to be deleted because of disuse (you can't remember how to do them), changes in how the skill is done that you haven't kept up with, or obsolescence (we don't use carbon paper or adding machines anymore)?

Update Your Skills Sort

Over time, the skills on this chart are likely to change. You may now appreciate skills that are currently in your Trash Heap. New skills may have replaced those on your Display Shelf.

Recombine

For this exercise, you'll want to enlist the help of two or three friends. Using your Skills Sort chart, pick a set of four skills. Brainstorm to create a list of every possible career that would utilize those skills. Be creative. Don't allow any limitations. Repeat with a second set of skills. Try for a third. Now, select careers that might interest you. Brainstorm how to move into them. Do some research about them, including looking at online hiring sites to see how each skill is described. Set up some informational interviews to learn more about how to move into the field.

Chapter 5

Tracking Your Life Purpose

If you've been tracking your career against your mission and vision, there will come a point where you realize that you've found out exactly what you are meant to be. You may not have taken the opportunity to retrace your steps and see what parts of that vision you have already realized or how your vision, mission, and goals come together to create a career where you feel like you've come home at last. For me, that career was coaching. It took me time to realize how long coaching had been part of my work and how to make it my primary focus.

One of the things that I learned early on when I was a Co-op coordinator is I am very good at helping people be better at things that I do not understand in the least. It's a bizarre talent, but nonetheless I could work with students who were accounting majors in accounting internships and help them become successful. I knew early on how to help people think about learning and think about what they were learning. That's a skill that I was able to use throughout my career, and that's what I was doing with co-op students and at HRA, both at OSDT and at the Academy, and at Transit.

I focused on the best way to learn a particular skill or skill set. What's going to help people really get this? They started calling me Doc because I was such a good script doctor, and I was a script doctor of training curricula. You could show me a curriculum and I could tell you exactly what was going to work and what wasn't going to work and figure out how to fix it. We would do run-throughs of the program and I would help people find better ways to present the material. I was facilitating learning. It's also, I think, part of what led me to coaching.

Teaching wasn't quite enough, and counseling was closer but not quite right either. When I discovered Thomas Leonard and heard him say that coaching was a sophisticated form of teaching, I knew that I'd found my home. Coaching was positive. Coaching had a teaching component. Coaching was transformative. Now, I just needed to find out where and how to learn to do this.

I was working at the Transit Authority when I made this discovery. Without understanding that I was doing this, many of the programs I developed grew out of transformative learning and coaching principles. I turned fifty and decided I'd had enough of this, and I quit. I quit my job and I never looked back. I might have a few regrets about my pension, but those were outweighed by mental and physical health issues. I said once again, okay, I'm going to set myself up as a consultant, but at least this time I knew what I wanted to be consulting on. So I decided to be a coach and consultant and do organizational development work because I had a good foundation in that now. I knew that I could do stress management, emotional intelligence, anger management, and trainer development and that I could continue my coach training and start coaching individuals.

I had a business partner, and we did some work together over the next couple of years. She had found me a part-time job with a friend of hers who ran a nonprofit. I worked there a couple of days a week, trying to be her executive coach and trying to get her organized. I've never had such a resistant client, and it's where I learned about solopreneurs. Solopreneurs cannot necessarily make the transition to be the boss of their business; she was one of those. She never made that transition and I never really did get her to but she was a great contact and I got some consulting work through her.

I got involved in an action learning project with a large pharmaceutical company. That was a delightful experience because I was training the facilitators to work with the small learning groups. At one point, they needed an extra facilitator, so I was facilitating a group of my own. I did that for about a year and a half. This was wonderful because this was group coaching at its best. I would go out there and over the months I would see these people change; there would be physical changes in these people. They would be looking better and standing taller and more self-confident, so it went back to the thing that I had been doing at Medgar Evers where I was working around self-esteem. I thought, *Aha, now I see how this works.*

After a while, I felt like I was so dragged into projects at my not-so-part-time job that I wasn't really focusing on building my own practice, so I decided that I was going to quit. My timing was impeccable; it was September 2001. My last day of work was 9/11 and, like everybody else in the city, I was just devastated. I went home; I didn't know what to do. My heart wasn't really in marketing at that point, and nobody was really looking to buy anything at that point either.

I had started to do some teaching at CoachVille. I started as a student at CoachVille and next thing I knew, I was a Community Coach, developing subject matter and teaching classes. I did some curriculum development including Energy Pattern coaching.

By 2001, I was still not fully functioning and was suffering from post-9/11 depression. I didn't know what I was going to do at all but I had to do something. I went to my old friends working for the Department of Personnel (now the Department of Citywide Administrative Services). I spoke with the head of the Bureau of Personnel Development and said, "I need a job. What am I going to do?" I had hired him as an intern at the beginning of his career. I also spoke with the director of training, who had been a colleague of mine for many years when I was still working there.

Shortly after we had this conversation, the Bureau put out a request for proposals looking for consultants to come in and do training, and I jumped on it. I got hired as a consultant and started doing curriculum development and training. At that time, the Citywide Department of Environmental Protection was under severe sanctions. A colleague and I developed training for them, and over two years we trained every manager and supervisor in the entire agency. We ended up with a team of people teaching the courses. Of course, I developed trainer development courses again, and designed a week-long advanced managerial program.

All this time, I kept on saying to the director that we needed coaching programs, the City needs coaching. The commissioner of the Human Resources Administration read an article in *The Wall Street Journal* about coaching and said, "We need some of this. We need this at HRA." He called in a couple of big consulting firms that do coaching and they gave him gorgeous proposals on glossy paper that would cost hundreds of thousands of dollars to implement. He decided to ask Citywide Training for a proposal. I was just waiting for a moment like this.

My proposal knocked the private firms out of the picture. It was better, it was considerably less expensive, and I had a team of coaches who had worked with HRA over a number of years. We didn't need to spend five months doing research to understand the needs of the population; we know the needs of the population.

At our presentation, the commissioner said, "What's this like?" I said, "Well, if it's okay, I'd like to coach you." He said, "Sure." So in this meeting for the whole team, I coached the commissioner.

He liked it; he did it. He saw that it could be very practical. We ran six cohorts of senior-level managers who each got fifteen sessions of coaching. They were wonderful people, and eventually we allowed some people to come back for a second round because they had said,

"We've grown, we've changed; now we need the next step." It was really successful and really rewarding. The idea of mixing self-esteem, personal development, and empowerment has been on my mind since the work that I did at Medgar Evers.

At some point, my partner and I had tried to sell a program to an organization called Strive that originally worked with men who had been incarcerated to try and help them be better fathers and help them find employment. At the time they didn't have anything. I got a call a couple of years later saying: We remember you and we loved your energy and we just got this grant. We're doing a program called LIFTT, Living for Today and Tomorrow. Would you please design the program for us and run it?

This was wonderful because this was coaching women who were disenfranchised. Either they'd been in jail or they'd been abused or they were substance abusers or simply didn't have any job skills. They were getting basic skills to succeed on the job. They were getting some skills in the basic program, but this was enhancing them and adding interpersonal and life management skills.

We started with life histories and skills identification. I developed materials for them, and we managed to somehow stretch the funds to run this program for three years. We had something like a 97 percent success rate, by which I mean 97 percent of the participants ended up either back in school or in a job by the end of this nine-week program.

In the meantime, my former business partner and I had written a book called *Get What You Need*. It was a career development book. I had all these materials and now I was really interested in what happens to women at midlife because a lot of these women just don't know what they want to do next but they know they want to do something. I started developing these materials into something called Mapping Midlife. I eventually revised the materials to become Life Blue Prints that address seven specific areas. Each of them has a separate workbook.

I was using skills that I had been using for most of my career – they had simply morphed over the years, over the positions, based on how my vision had become more refined. This is a common pattern in serial careerists. It may be your pattern. That makes this a good point to review your personal vision and goals.

Updated Skills and Obstacles list

Skills and Assets	Potential Obstacles
Solid Foundation	~~Learned to stay in the background~~
Resilience	~~Loss of trust~~
Working with children	Low self-esteem
Creativity	Poor self-image
Writing	Needing external validation
Typing and filing	~~Poor typing skills~~
Wardrobe planning/coordination	Weight issues
Public speaking ability	Hate public speaking
Curriculum development	
Career coaching	
Conference planning	
Leadership	
Coordination	
Writing	
Personal Development Coaching	
Executive Coaching	
Teaching Coaching	
Mentoring	

What's important for you in this part of my story?

You may find, as I did, that a series of jobs brought satisfaction and growth yet still left you with a feeling that something was lacking. As you continue to learn and grow through a succession of positions, you will become increasingly sure about what speaks to your heart. Go for it! Even after you find the perfect field, you may still move through a variety of experiences within that field.

For the curious and restless group: Review your career trajectory in terms of your vision, mission, and goals. Have your careers fit into a pattern that brought you closer to your vision? If not, you may want to review and possibly reset your goals. If, like me, you see a pattern of getting closer, what are your next steps? If you feel you're not getting closer, it's time to look at what's stopping you.

For the mid- to late-career group: Are there ways that you still want to grow? Can you do this where you are or add activities that complete the puzzle? Is it time to move on?

For the late entry or re-entry group: Reflect on your vision in terms of your updated life history. What has been most important to you? How can you use your skills to realize that vision?

Strategy 5: Be Patient; Stay Open to Miracles and New Possibilities

Exercises

These exercises help you redefine your mission and goals and explore the barriers created by conflicting intentions.

Eulogy or Testimonial Revisited
Rewrite Your Eulogy

As a serial careerist, you may want to do this exercise periodically and keep all the previous versions for reference. You may discover that you have a core vision, as I did, that plays out in many ways, or that your vision changes over time. This will, of course, have an impact on your goals and may mean a change of path. Change is wonderful – and best when it's planned. Yes, spontaneity can be planned, especially when you are aware of your long- and short-term goals.

If you have your original visioning exercise, have it handy for comparison but avoid reading it before you complete the exercise. You'll be comparing them. Imagine that you are writing your own eulogy. If you find the idea of writing a eulogy upsetting or threatening, picture yourself writing a testimonial being given about you at a big awards banquet honoring your lifetime achievements. Find a quiet, private space and something to write on. Turn off the television. Get rid of any distractions. Take a few deep breaths. Clear your mind of other concerns. If you wish, close your eyes.

Imagine a room full of people who love you who have come together to celebrate your life. Imagine that you have accomplished everything that you ever hoped to do. Your every dream has been fulfilled. Everyone who is important to you is gathered to talk about the wonderful person you were and about your many accomplishments. If you listen, you can hear the speakers. Write down what they are saying about you.

What are all the things you have accomplished? Have you traveled? Where? What have you created? Have you written or painted or played the flute or knitted or gardened? Did you cook for friends? Volunteer at a soup kitchen? Teach someone something? Send perfect postcards or birthday cards? Write as quickly as you can and don't censor your writing. When you have written as much as you can, put it aside overnight. Now go back to your eulogy and read it very slowly. What did you leave out? Make any additions you feel are important.

Update Your Goals

Go back over your eulogy and highlight your accomplishments, then create a separate list of these accomplishments. What will you need to do to make all of the things that you heard a reality? Those accomplishments you have yet to achieve represent potential goals. They will serve as the basis for planning your life goals.

Review Your Values

Go back one more time and highlight the things people said about you. Look at these in relation to your accomplishments and generate a list of things that you value or that represent your values (e.g., family ties, hard work, friendship).

This exercise will help you create an overall guide for your life.

Revisiting Your Personal Vision and Mission Statement

Vision Statement

Your personal vision statement should describe what you ultimately envision the greater purpose of your life to be, in terms of growth, values, contributions to society, etc. As you grow and change, your vision and mission may also change. Self-reflection is a vital activity if you want to develop a meaningful vision.

Once you have redefined your vision, you can begin to develop strategies for moving toward that vision. Part of this includes the development of a mission statement. What do you want for the rest of your life? Take a few minutes to write down your personal vision. This will be based on your goals and values.

Mission Statement

Vision statements and mission statements are very different. Your mission statement is the vision translated into written form. It is a concrete expression of how you will bring your revised vision to life. A mission statement should be a short and concise statement of goals and priorities. Your mission statement should be a concise statement of strategy, and it should fit with your vision. The mission should answer three questions:

1. What will I do?
2. How will I do it?
3. For whom will I do it?

What will I do? This question should be answered in terms of what are the concrete and psychological needs that you want to fulfill.

How will I do it? This question captures the more technical elements.

For whom will I do it? The answer to this question is also vital, as it will help you focus your efforts.

Review Your Goals

What do you now see as the overall goal of your life? This is generally called an overarching goal. Think of this overarching goal as your mental picture of your career/life trajectory. It's helpful to review your goals periodically to eliminate those that are either completed or no longer relevant and to add new ones.

Write down the biggest current goal you can think of – a real stretch goal – something that will definitely expand your comfort zone. This is your overarching goal, not dissimilar from your personal mission statement, simply a bit more refined – more specific. Then, you will become even more specific as you plan out your sub-goals that support the overarching goal.

Perhaps the simplest way to bring your goal from general to specific is to use a proven goal-setting formula: S-M-A-R-T goals. Check your goal against the S-M-A-R-T criteria and tweak away until it's as clear and strong as possible. When you design a home, if you don't have a really good sense of what the completed building looks like, it will be hard to plan the individual rooms. The criteria are described below.

Specific – as detailed as possible

Measurable – criteria that will indicate progress toward and completion of the goal

Achievable – Is this something that you can actually do?

Realistic – Can this actually happen?

Timely/Time-framed – How long will this take? Is this the right goal for right now?

What's Holding You Back?

How often do you feel like that mythical beast from *Dr. Doolittle* – the PushmePullyou? You really want to take that next step to move forward in some part of your life only to find that it's as if your feet are stuck in the mud. You want something, but part of you wants something else that may even be the complete opposite. So you go nowhere.

People usually take steps to meet their desires or carry out their intentions unless there is some internal force or energy that is holding them back. We call these conflicting desires or conflicting intentions. It's like having two energy forces pulling you in two different directions. You are stuck in the middle of this tug-of-war and it's probably making you very, very tired.

When we know what we want and work toward that goal, life goes along smoothly, but when we run into barriers, we need to stop and do some work.

The barriers that stop us in our tracks are self-imposed, so we need strategies to break through those artificial walls and get what we want. You may think that your barriers are outside yourself, but, really, they are in your own mind – in your attitude and in the reasons you tell yourself you can't have what you want. As Henry Ford said, "Whether you think you can or you can't, you're right!"

So, this whole process of moving forward begins with clearing the self-imposed barriers in our lives that keep us from moving forward.

Wake-up Call

The first step is a wake-up call. This is that little aha moment when you realize that you aren't getting the results you want. You begin to realize that something is holding you back. What's something you've said you want to do but are not actually doing?

What's Stopping You?

Most of us carry out our intentions unless there is some underlying issue that conflicts with our stated desire. If we look at the physics underlying attraction, we understand that *everything* is made up of energy. This includes thoughts, actions, intentions, things, and circumstances. They are all made up of energy. So, our desires have energy that causes things to happen or come to us. We still need to take action to make things happen, but even when this involves hard work, it isn't a continuous struggle. However, when things *don't* happen, there is almost always an unseen or unspoken intention that has more energy than our desire.

These conflicting intentions represent mixed messages we give ourselves and often come from old messages from our past that we are carrying forward.

Here's an example: A writer felt that achieving bestseller status would mean she would stop working and sit around eating chocolates. She's an award-winning poet and still working hard. The image she's holding is of what her parents have done, not how she has chosen to lead her life. Still, the conflict between wanting success and fearing success will ruin her life, holds her back.

Reality Check

People act differently on intentions based on how important the intention is to them. Do a quick check to be sure that this intention is important to you. Is it a distraction? What do you *really* want to do?

You mentioned that you want to work on _____. *What have you done so far? Has that been hard or easy? What are you not* doing?

How have you tried to get going? Is that working for you? Why not?

Clearing Conflicting Thoughts

Everything that happens is a collaboration between you and the universe. Intentions are energy.

All of our intentions are prone to being sabotaged by conflicting intentions, especially the intentions that are really meaningful to us.

Restate your intention. Then outline, in no more than five steps, how you plan to achieve that intention. Are you acting on this plan or stuck?

Sit with your plan for a while. Examine each step by asking the following questions:

- What's really going on here?

- What story am I telling myself?
- Is that true?
- What evidence do I have to support that?

If you find evidence to support your story, perhaps this is the wrong intention, or perhaps the story is based on faulty interpretations. Now ask:

- Where does my story come from?
- What might be a reframe or an alternate explanation?

Moving Forward

We get conflicting intentions from our past conditioning and socialization. Stories that protected us in the past might no longer serve us.

When you have an intention, whether it's to get a close parking space (in the moment, it's easy; it happens or it doesn't but there's little or no baggage) or get ten new clients (longer term, future-oriented,) the next thing you want to do is be very aware of the conflicts.

You want your conflicting intentions to come to the surface. Then you can do something about them. You want to design an environment that causes your conflicting intentions to come to the surface. This is the thing they never teach you about in an affirmations class!

Dr. Susan R. Meyer

Chapter 6

Overcoming Fear and Depression – Rollercoaster Times

In the first chapter, I talked about patterns that develop in childhood that stay with us throughout life. Some of my most negative circled back all too often. Therapy and coaching have helped me recognize them when they crop up, and I've developed some pretty good coping mechanisms, but sometimes nothing seemed to help. When this happens, it's time to deal head-on with fear. Much of what you'll find here is a tale of avoiding that fear or taking temporary measures. It becomes clear, though, that, while temporary fixes may let you get back to some level of function, it isn't until you are ready for the pain of facing your fears that you can fully become the person you are meant to be.

What I've learned is that postponing the hard work on yourself means making the same mistake over and over again. If you want to stop being a people pleaser – if you want to stop believing all that bad press you're writing about yourself – you can't avoid the deep thinking, the search for what's really true, and the reframing that lets you move on. I see clients early in their careers who are in jobs that are eating them alive. "I'll wait a few more months to see if I get that promotion," they say. "It's not so bad," they say.

We look at the fears that are keeping them stuck. Some are brave and begin the hard work. Some aren't yet ready – and even the best coach in the universe can't create that readiness – and they will live in the pain that they know instead of looking at how the pain is stopping them. If you are on the fence, it's time to jump. It doesn't have to be a big jump or a deep dive. Start with gently stirring the waters or taking a tiny hop and see how that feels.

Early Warning Signs

I spent a lot of time in my mid-twenties shaping my life around pleasing mostly fictitious men by proving how strong and independent I was to guys who were no longer in my life. I would envision them reemerging and, upon discovering how strong and independent I was, proposing to me so we could go off to happily-ever-after-ville. I'd go to the supermarket thinking, M_ will be so impressed that I can carry my own groceries, totally ignoring the fact that a) most people can manage to carry their groceries and b) M_ was happily touring Europe with his wife. I had an amazing interior (fantasy) life. It almost compensated for the gaps in my real life.

For quite a while, this was enough. I was mostly carefree and just a little lonely. I was happy enough working as an assistant teacher in Greenwich Village. Theater and movies were cheap and there were enough political/protest activities to keep everyone busy and surrounded by like-thinking people all the time. The thing was, at the end of the day I was still alone and unhappy. I didn't realize that I was depressed until, while on a walk with my preschool group, I stopped dead in the middle of the street. I was frozen in place. Another teacher had to physically prod me into motion.

That scared me enough to send me straight to a therapist. It didn't take long for me to realize that I knew more about counseling than he did, but he did help me surface some of my core issues and get back to functioning better. As I reflect on this, I'm sure that I chose him because he was safe and not sufficiently skilled to get me to really face my issues. I wanted a Band-Aid, not surgery.

Through most of my adult life I didn't feel good enough. I would prove myself again and again, but, even when I was getting accolades for my work, for my cooking, for my leadership, it never seemed real. Off and on I'd found someone to shore me up when I needed help. Often, this was short term. Not the best solution, but it was something. A quick fix might be better than a glass of wine at the end of the day, but it may not last much longer and it doesn't make that baggage you're carrying any lighter. I didn't think about this until all that baggage crashed down around me.

At some point, if your underlying issues keep rising to the surface and disrupting your life, you need professional help. When I was in my twenties, there weren't a lot of choices – and even fewer affordable options. Now, there are coaches and therapists to fit everyone's individual needs and budgets. There are practices like yoga and meditation. There are spiritual groups, retreats, Zen and Buddhist practices, churches, and synagogues with a wide range of support groups, all available to get you through hard times and to help you create deeper meaning in your life. Quick Rule: When in doubt, seek help out.

Always, always, always have a support network. Always know that you have someone to speak with. Honest friends will tell you when your issues are too big or too complicated for them and will support you in your search for a coach or therapist. They'll also be there for you every step of the way. Don't get to the point where you are immobilized. I've been there more than once and can tell you it's not worth it. When you feel the pain, don't tamp it down and keep on going. It will just grow. Acknowledge the pain and get someone to help you through it.

I was stubborn. I felt that I'd been taking care of myself since I was eight and didn't need any help. I was sure I could ignore the pain. After all, I had evidence. I had survived the loss of my mother. I never realized that I didn't properly mourn her. I didn't mourn her because I wasn't allowed to. Everyone was very stoic. No one wanted to talk about her. So, when my father died, I mimicked what I'd learned. It was in the middle of exam week and instead of staying home I insisted on going in for an exam. I remember telling my best friend that she had to tell me every joke she knew so that I wouldn't cry. With so many years of sitting on my feelings, it took that complete mid-street stop for me to admit that I needed help.

Maintain your support circle. At every stage of life, as the song goes, "You've gotta have friends." We all need people to talk with on a regular basis – people who share our stories, laugh at our jokes, listen when we need a listener, cheer on our projects, keep us on track. Your circle of friends requires maintenance, though. I've learned to keep track of when I've last spoken with or spent time with my circle and will schedule time with each of them.

Although this may seem artificial, it's all too easy to let relationships slip when you become deeply involved in a project or when you're depressed. You may not even realize that you're withdrawing. I didn't. I mentioned earlier that when I was working on my dissertation I cut myself off from everyone. I did the same thing when I was working on my first book. Once I got into the flow of writing, I didn't want to be distracted by anything or anyone. I didn't answer the phone or the door. I finished both projects in record time, but it cost me friendships. Once you become isolated in this way, it's hard to rebuild.

Implosion

There came a time that I found myself on a roller coaster so fast that I couldn't catch my breath. I was at the peak of my career. I had a solid consulting practice. I developed and managed the first internal coaching program within a City agency. I was teaching coaching at NYU. I had time and money to travel. I had good friends, although they were mostly scattered across the country.

I had gone to an event commemorating the life of my favorite professor and dissertation sponsor and had a conversation with a former student. When I was praising him for his accomplishments, he told me that it was because – looking me straight in the eye – that it was because he was standing on the shoulders of giants. Wow. I was floating. Soon after this, he asked me to join the faculty of the Columbia Coaching Certificate Program. This was a dream come true. I knew that Teachers College needed to have a coaching program. Both doctoral programs in our department had transformative learning as a major focus – what better home for coaching? I had pushed for the program. I finally got one of my fellow coaches to push my former student to start thinking about this and, while interdepartmental politics kept me off the program's faculty, I followed its growth closely. Finally! I would be part of this.

You may have noticed that all this does not include success in my personal life. This is where you can see how the parts of your life that are not in great shape and the baggage that keeps them the way they are will, at some point, come back to bite you. Big-time.

I decided that I felt great about my life – didn't even miss being in a relationship. I didn't, after all, need anyone. In fact, I saw this as a positive shift from trying to please a fictitious life partner. Then, everything unraveled. The City got a new mayor, who hired new commissioners who instantly tore down all the programs that their predecessors put in place. That meant the end of my contract with New York City's Human Resources Administration (HRA) – my biggest client. My Buddhist group broke up, ending what had become a strong spiritual connection and source of support.

I was depressed. I thought that I should have been able to do something to save the coaching program. My income disappeared. I no longer had a City contract, so I didn't have that as a source of future employment. I was pretty much broke. There was a lot of shuffling at NYU and I didn't get any new classes. I got turned down for unemployment benefits because I had a website, and therefore a potential source of income.

But I still had my dream spot teaching in the Columbia Coaching Certificate Program. My dream quickly turned into a nightmare as

I discovered that as much as I loved the program, I simply wasn't a good fit. It required being structured – and I'm not a structured person. It required teaching in a way that was antithetical to all that I see as my teaching strengths. It didn't help that I hadn't had enough time to really digest the program in its entirety before being thrown in and that because the program was quarterly there was too much time between repetitions. It also didn't help that I wasn't assigned a mentor and was expected to somehow know everything that was in the curriculum.

The biggest issue was that I was trying too hard to be someone I wasn't. It reminded me of when I worked for employment agencies. It was important to look, dress, and act a certain way that they called "corporate crisp." I did my best, but it wasn't me. I remember a guy at a party laughing when I told him that I was dressed in my best corporate crisp. His response? "You couldn't be corporate crisp no matter how hard you tried." Same thing. I couldn't get the rhythm. The language, the style. Instead of thinking that this simply wasn't me, I took it as a failure that I couldn't remold myself. I was disappointing my former student and I was disappointing myself. I had to resign. It was a hard way to be reminded that I needed to honor my personal values and style and not try to be someone that I wasn't.

I was convinced that all of this was my fault, and I was a total failure. Just to reinforce this, during the time I was teaching in the Columbia Program I took on a new coaching client. Pretty much everyone I knew had turned down working with this agency. A fellow coach, who worked with them in a different capacity and couldn't also manage this, thought I might be able to help the agency. Of course, my Superwoman mindset kicked right in, and I accepted the contract. Huge mistake.

While the executive team proclaimed their desire for open, authentic communication, what they actually wanted, individually, was to never share anything but that everyone else would share with them and allow them to comment. That was the least of their problems. Instead of seeing the experience as a losing battle, though, I took it as a personal failure. This and the Columbia failure overlapped. Clearly, I felt, I was stupid and worthless. I hadn't tried hard enough. I was wallowing in negative thinking and self-pity rather than concentrating on my strengths, eliminating false beliefs, and starting over.

Unless you are a professional contortionist, don't twist yourself into knots to meet someone else's idea of who you should be. I see this in current clients who work in heavy command and control organizations. Their bosses grew up in environments where shouting and abuse, insanely heavy workloads, and ridiculous hours were the norm. When they questioned this pattern, they were told that if it was good enough for the boss, they shouldn't be complaining. These younger managers, though, are a different age cohort and have very different feelings about the workplace. These clients are deciding that, no, it doesn't have to be that way and are getting good results without twisting themselves into someone they can't even recognize. And they can sleep at night.

I was drifting into depression before I lost the HRA contract. I just didn't realize it. I was gaining weight, sleeping a lot, avoiding people, not doing anything. At first, I thought it was just aging. I was, after all, past sixty-five. Then I decided it was medical, since anemia, thyroid medication, diabetes, and blood pressure medications all contributed to depression. It was time to see if an antidepressant would help – almost all of my friends had been on them for years.

I tried a low-level antidepressant that never made me feel better. It turned out to be most often used with cancer patients to increase their appetite as much as to improve their mood. Not the best choice for someone already eating anything in sight. I discovered that a friend had the same experience. She'd buy a cake to have dessert for the week, then pick up a second one "just in case," then go home and eat both of them. We both opted out of that med pretty quickly.

For a couple of months, I did nothing. I sat at home. I watched really bad television. I overate. I didn't shower too often. When I finally couldn't stand the way I looked or smelled I decided to do something about it. I went back to my old coach for a while and I started coaching myself. I took a couple of amazingly healing writing workshops.

It wasn't quick and it wasn't easy. I ditched the antidepressant. I joined a gym to have access to a treadmill. I ate less and better. I forced myself to get out of the house and spend time with other people. I reconnected with friends I'd ignored for a long time. I did the self-work necessary to eliminate false beliefs and reengage in positive thinking. I took a long, hard look at what I wanted for this next phase of my life and created a new set of goals and an action plan.

Skills and Assets	Potential Obstacles
Solid Foundation	~~Learned to stay in the background~~
Resilience	~~Loss of trust~~
Working with children	Low self-esteem
Creativity	Poor self-image
Writing	Needing external validation
Typing and filing	~~Poor typing skills~~
Wardrobe planning/coordination	Weight issues
Public speaking ability	Hate public speaking
Curriculum development	Fear
Career coaching	
Conference planning	
Leadership	
Coordination	
Writing	
Personal Development Coaching	
Executive Coaching	
Teaching Coaching	
Mentoring	

What's important for you in this part of my story?

Create an early warning system for yourself. If you ignore every warning sign and wait until you bottom out, it can take years to repair and heal. If you catch yourself before you start to isolate...or stop showering...or substitute chocolate for people...you can reclaim your life.

If you put off seeking help, you will get caught in an inescapable repetitive cycle. Over time, this may have an impact on your career choices – you may settle for less than you deserve or postpone making changes. There are programs and practitioners in every price range and covering a wide range of issues. Find someone or something that best suits your needs. Reach out to your friends. Get out into the world. Depression can kill.

This applies to all three categories (the curious, mid- to late-career, and late entry or re-entry).

Strategy 6: Dealing with Fear

Exercises

These exercises will help you find support and help you deal with self-limiting beliefs.

Review Your Support Circle

Regularly review your support circle. You may be surprised at how long some people have been in your circle or may find that you barely remember a name or two. Take a moment to thank those few for all they've done before you delete their names and add new ones.

These are the people who help you get through life. They're the ones who help you make hard decisions and recover from disasters and take care of yourself and rise to greatness. You'll want a second chart, by the way, that shows you who you support. Refresh your charts twice a year to be sure that the people you have in place are still part of your life in the same way. Your support network will be right there to help you if life becomes too overwhelming and you need more help than they can give. They'll help you research your options, evaluate your choices, and make sure that you show up for your appointments.

Catastrophize

This is a "what if" exercise that relieves anxiety. By the time you finish it, you may be laughing at your problem or will at least have some possible courses of action.

Imagine the worst-case scenario of an issue that is depressing you or keeping you up at night. Write it down. Then, answer the questions.

Issue Example: I might lose my job.

1. On a scale of 1–10, how likely is that to happen?

2. If it does happen? What will you do?

Based on what you've said you'll do, answer the same two questions. Repeat these five to seven times. How do you feel about the final answer?

Obsessing Break

Sometimes, we can't get a situation out of our mind. This is a technique an actor I know would use when he was waiting to hear about an audition. He had a habit of rubbing his hands on his thighs when he was anxious and was wearing through his jeans, something he could ill afford. He started creating obsession breaks. He would set his timer for five minutes and allow himself to obsess about his situation. When the timer went off, he would force himself to move on to something else. I find that this works best if, when the timer goes off, you have a change of location or dive into some chore you've been avoiding.

Puff Balls

When you are feeling depressed or dealing with an old fear or pain, this can be useful. This works best if you can do it with a friend.

Describe the situation that is upsetting you. Go into detail. Find something odd about the story. Expand on that. Can you find something strange or silly in the story? For example, threats of sexual abuse are in no way comical, yet I used this technique to deal with one. As I told the story, I began to realize that the threat was repeatedly worded in a way that somehow sounded chivalrous. With each retelling, it became more exaggerated. With the help of my friend, a fellow coach, I was able to turn the situation into a puff ball. I pictured myself blowing the puff ball away. It's been ten years since I last felt the impact of those threats.

Lists

Sometimes, we need concrete visual reminders of the impact we've had. This is especially useful when you're having an "I'm nobody" moment or when you're feeling alone or unloved.

Make two lists. One will be all your accomplishments with evidence. The second will be all the people who like or admire you, also with evidence. Keep them someplace where you can see them whenever you need reassurance.

Finally, there are excellent coaches, counselors, therapists, and psychiatrists out there. Speak to a few candidates to find the best match for you. Coaching is often short-term – at least three months, generally not more than a year. Many clients develop lifelong relationships with their coach and reengage in the process as needed. Never be ashamed to get professional help. Always use reputable referral sources and have an introductory session.

Dr. Susan R. Meyer

Chapter 7

Reemerging: Retirement Redefined

This is a little like the screeching halt described earlier, but for many it's more like a slow drift. You may not notice the losses until you've bottomed out. For some of you, there may be a point in your career where you simply feel that you need to step out for a while.

After everything seemed to come unraveled, I relied on my social security and pension and took on any small project that would bring in a little cash while I was looking for what was next. I did faculty teaching evaluations for the Stern School at NYU; I did some curriculum revisions for a friend who has a coaching school. I evaluated candidates for coach certification for my professional association.

None of these were especially satisfying. For many years, I had been passionate about curriculum design. It came to me easily and it felt like figuring out puzzles. At this point, I found it neither challenging nor satisfying. In part, this shift probably occurred when I took an assignment to develop a curriculum for accountants a few years earlier. It was another of those between-things periods and I needed the money. Now, I know nothing about accounting. I'm a good enough researcher to find all the information I needed to create a curriculum, but none of it was fun. Just to make this a perfect experience, my back went out and I had to construct a sort of lectern so that I could type standing up.

Remember the skill sort exercise? This was a perfect example of using what I call recycle skills when you need to. These are survival skills. Sometimes, you'll need them to get through rough spots. With this in mind, this is a good time to revisit your skills chart. It may be that you'll need those file cabinet and recycle skills in your next transition. You may also find that something in the trash heap is no longer something you're good at and hate – you may feel differently about it.

Faculty evaluation was a mixed blessing. Again, it utilized skills I was not using on a regular basis at this point. Some of the courses were fascinating and I learned a lot both in terms of the content – marketing film, for example – and the variety of teaching styles. Math-phobic me was mesmerized by a ninety-year-old professor who made the subject fascinating and was the best example of teaching excellence I saw in the two years I did evaluations. He moved around the room, knew everyone's name, and asked excellent questions. The challenge was twofold. One was that some professors were not open to feedback. The harder challenge was staying awake in 7:00 – 9:00 p.m. classes on boring topics.

For a year or so I evaluated certification candidates for my professional organization. When this started taking up more time than it was worth and I had better options, I stepped away from this, but the door is still open if I want to go back.

Pay close attention to your finances. Know what's the least you can live on. Squirrel money away on a regular basis. Even in hard times, I use a trick I learned from another consultant. Stash away five-dollar bills. You won't miss them and they accumulate quickly. That consultant financed her move to Austin. I used my first stash to take a vacation in the south of France.

I knew exactly what I wanted next. I wanted to build a practice around helping people who were stuck in their lives figure out what was next. While I was figuring out how to make that a reality, I wanted a coaching practice where I was working for an organization that would do the marketing and provide a regular flow of clients. I found what, for me, is the perfect organization. I have a steady roster of ten to fourteen clients through them. I enjoy the work and it has allowed me time for another passion – writing – and time to build my private practice. For serial careerists, multiple part-time careers are an excellent option. They provide variety. They allow us a way to use varied skills. They allow us to structure our time in a way that works for us, including taking tme off at will.

What's important for you in this part of my story?

It's good for a serial careerist to have an arsenal of jobs like these for lean periods. Or to utilize sites like Fiverr to find freelance opportunities. Pick assignments that you can easily move away from and can go back to when you need them. For all three groups (curious, mid- to late-career, late entry, or re-entry) keep close track of your finances. Ask your friends for leads. Let them know that you're looking for work. Have a cluster of part-time jobs,

Skills and Assets	Potential Obstacles
Solid Foundation	~~Learned to stay in the background~~
Resilience	~~Loss of trust~~
Working with children	Low self-esteem
Creativity	Poor self-image
Writing	Needing external validation
Typing and filing	~~Poor typing skills~~
Wardrobe planning/coordination	Weight issues
Public speaking ability	Hate public speaking
Curriculum development	
Career coaching	
Conference planning	
Leadership	
Coordination	
Writing	
Personal Development Coaching	

Strategy 7: Recombine Skills
Strategy 8: Reassess, Prioritize

Exercises

Dream/Brainstorm

Go back to your skills chart. Pick two skills from your Display Shelf. Imagine that everything is possible (because, in fact, it is). Create a list of every possible way you can use those skills – every possible job or volunteer experience. Great brainstorming involves doing something called breaking set. Most lists will begin with fairly obvious choices. You'll want to get beyond those, though. Keep listing possibilities until you get to some that sound ridiculous. Add those to your list!

You have now broken set – moved beyond the known into the unknown. Earlier, I described a woman who thought that she was going to be a Teacher's Aide and ended up being elected to the state assembly. Break point for her was, in considering alternate careers that used her skills, coming up with circus clown. This got her thinking about public-facing careers and a future in politics.

Research

Pick your top three or four new possibilities to research. The research has three parts.

Explore the field

What, exactly, does work in this field look like? Where can you do this? What does it pay? Can you find stories about people who do this work? What has the most appeal for you? Are there tradeoffs or drawbacks? After doing the research, does this still appeal to you? If yes, put it on the short list for the next part of the exercise. If not, does your research suggest new possibilities? If yes, explore them. If not, move on to exploration.

Explore getting experience

Research ways to try out your top contenders. There are internships. There are volunteer experiences. There are work-cations that give you a short-term opportunity to try out something new.

Plan

Check your time and finances. Know how many experiments you can create for yourself

Experiment and Document

Go for it! Document each experience as you move through it. This will help you know whether this transition is one you want now or want to consider for the future. It may also open up ideas about related fields or aspects of this field that you have not previously considered.

Chapter 8

My Fuller Life History and Insights

You've seen segments of my life history throughout the earlier chapters. Those segments are designed to give you a context for the exercises, to focus on what to consider at different points in a career and to demonstrate how skills may change over time. This fuller version provides an opportunity to see what a life history looks like as a whole. It also underscores how the insights that shape our lives emerge along the way. Feel free to skim, stopping to focus on the insights. They're clearly marked along the way.

I see my life as a series of contradictions and a constant balancing act. I consider myself to be both a very successful professional and an underachiever. I am the product of at least two generations of contradiction and conflict, so I come by it naturally.

My paternal grandparents were an odd combination. My grandmother always said her parents were British Jews. Decades later we found out that they were actually Prussian Jews who spent a brief time in England and that my great-grandparents were actually born in Toronto and Kansas City. The fiction remained, though. Her father – a jeweler – was the poor relation of an upper-middle-class family. They had only one servant. As near as I can tell, his wife was a professional invalid. My grandmother completed high school – unusual in 1918 – and went on to the Katharine Gibbs Secretarial School. She was an executive secretary most of her life.

No one ever praised my grandmother while she was growing up; no one ever told her that she was pretty, so when a handsome young man climbed over the seat in a movie theater and told her she was beautiful, she married him. There's a long history of not feeling good enough in the family. Gram overcompensated by being brash. Her mother compensated by being a professional invalid. Her father was so insecure about the switch from platinum to gold in his business that he killed himself.

My grandfather's family were lower-class Germans. He managed to finish third grade before becoming a bricklayer. His father was an upholsterer and his mother cleaned houses. Mostly, though, his family drank. My only memory of my great-grandfather is of him sitting in a big, wingback chair asking for another beer. My grandfather and his brothers were all alcoholics. One was downright mean; the second was quiet and sweet. My grandfather was handsome and charming right up to the point where he became loud and mean. Although he had been a foreman and was sent to Bermuda to build military installations, his construction career ended as he aged out of being able to do heavy labor and as building construction changed. He went through a series of jobs that relied on his natural charm, including selling novelty advertising items (cocktail napkins, matchbooks) to businesses. He bred exotic fish and was a fixture at pet shows. He claimed to be personal friends with Leo, the MGM lion. With my grandmother's help, he wrote articles about breeding fish. Somehow, my grandparents managed to stay married, survive the Depression, and raise three sons to adulthood.

My maternal grandparents were second-generation Italian immigrants. My great-grandmother put all her sons' names in a hat, the legend goes, and drew the name of the one son that all the other children would work to put through college. My grandfather was the lucky winner and eventually completed both a law degree and a doctorate in chemistry. His first wife, his childhood sweetheart, died of tuberculosis, shortly before her thirtieth birthday, when my mother was eight years old. This left her with lifelong scars that carried over to affect me. His second wife, who had been his housekeeper, transformed herself from German hausfrau to the perfect Italian wife to please my grandfather, but he never stopped talking about his first wife, whom we started calling "the blessed sainted Mary," and his son and daughter never accepted their stepmother.

Insight: *There were contradictory messages about the role of women and about praise that cycled back several times in my life. The issue of seeking praise especially would cause me difficulties for decades. Although I loved my mother's stepmother, my mother's attitude may have colored my feelings about my own stepmother.*

My parents met while working on their high school literary magazine. When my dad was accepted to the Agriculture School at Cornell, my mother followed him there. Mom was supposed to study chemistry and fulfill her father's desire to set her up with her own analysis business. She had other ideas, mainly to not let my father out of her sight. Dad's plan was to be a writer, not a farmer. We discovered a letter he wrote to Mom telling her to let Kurt Vonnegut know that he planned to be back in time to beat Kurt in the next literary competition. Their plans were disrupted by World War II. They had a small wedding before he shipped out to Europe and managed to create me during a weekend leave in Madison, Wisconsin. Mom's girlfriends took turns being my "second father."

Mom never went back to class, but Dad finished college when the war ended. The college converted what may have been chicken coops into Vetsburg, housing for all the Veteran families, and there we lived until Dad graduated. After, Dad completed school and we moved around a few times before settling in suburban Philadelphia, where he became a technical writer. We settled into an early pattern of moving that lasted, for me, until I was thirteen. For the next few years, though, I had an idyllic childhood, with a small close-knit group of neighborhood children to play with, art lessons, Brownie Scouts, a big, beautiful collie, and, when I was seven, a baby brother.

Those years in Hatboro saved me by getting me off to a good start. They established strength and independence. I felt loved. I was a free spirit, a leader, and an artist. I had yet to know loss or fear. I loved and trusted my parents, and even when things didn't work out as planned, the trust remained. For example, when my father was teaching me how to ride my bike, things didn't go as planned. He taught me how to balance but forgot about braking and was a little vague on steering. The first time he let go of the seat, I sailed along proudly and promptly steered right into a ditch. Luckily, I missed the cinder blocks at the bottom of the ditch and emerged shaken but relatively unscathed. My father was beside himself. I never thought about his role in this, and my complete trust in him never wavered. I got back on the bike and tried again. I had that same level of trust for all the adults in my life.

As I got older and things fell apart, I learned about pain and meanness and untrustworthy people. I withdrew and hid. I felt like everything that was wrong was my fault. But still, somewhere in there was that core of strength and the memory of that little girl, and I know it helped me survive and eventually heal. There are lessons and skills learned in your early childhood that may get you through the worst of times. There may be other lessons that will always be demons. List and remember your core strengths. List and address the demons. Your strengths and your demons will be part of every choice you ever make. You may need to decide how much pain or discomfort you are willing to take on in order to do something that you are passionate about.

Insight: *A strong early foundation creates resilience. In reviewing this life history, I realized how often I bounced back to this freedom*

and innocence. I was also able to see when and where I lost that atti-
tude so that eventually I was able to work my way out of depression.

Shortly after my brother's birth, we moved to a townhouse in a more urban area near Newark, New Jersey. For most of my life, starting with the move from Pennsylvania to New Jersey, I've always felt like an outsider. Moving so many times meant a series of adjustments – learning how to get along with new kids, trying to figure out what was going on in school. Kids are the harshest critics and don't take kindly to anything that is even a little different. The new kid always stands out, and if there's anything different about that kid, it becomes (or feels like it becomes) almost impossible to fit in.

Even before this, I'd learned that standing out or letting people know what you knew wasn't always a good idea. The first day of Vacation Bible Camp, when I was probably six, the campers were singing "Onward Christian Soldiers" as we moved from the sanctuary to our groups. Somehow I knew the words, and the counselor was so impressed that she made me stay until the end of the hymn. This meant that I didn't leave with my group – they didn't know the words – and afterwards no one helped me find them. By the time I was in the right place I was embarrassed to be coming in late and behind on the activity.

The move to New Jersey was an uncomfortable transition for me. In what I much later understood as a racist gesture, my parents put me in a Catholic school to avoid the integrated public school. Being the only non-Catholic in my first school in New Jersey made fitting in hard. I'd never even seen a nun before, and now my world was ruled by them. I had never been inside a Catholic church.

I did not understand any of the catechism we were required to learn. The subjects were different. Worst of all, soon after we moved, my mother became ill. I was the only child with a sick mother, the only child with a housekeeper, the only one who hadn't learned the Palmer method or the times tables. The only thing I did well was reading. And still, I often got in trouble because I read so fast that I was always ahead of my group. More than once, I got put into the slow group because Sister Martin Elizabeth never realized that I was a chapter ahead.

I didn't understand some of the rituals, either. The other children were putting crosses at the top of their papers and JMJ beneath that. When I finally discovered that this meant Jesus, Mary, Joseph I got obsessed and kept adding more initials –JMJPHMWMW – (Jesus, Mary, Joseph, please help me with my work) until Sister scolded me for messing up my paper. I was always out of step.

This was the beginning of a pattern of uncomfortable transitions. I learned early to be quiet and stay in the background for as long as I could. I was always trying to fit in and never quite figuring it out. I went from being the ringleader to the shy kid in the corner. It was a pattern that stayed with me through most of my life.

My mother's illness gave me my first exposure to people of color. She became so obsessed with the idea that she would die and my father would marry his housekeeper that we only hired Black women – supposedly to rule out the possibility of romance. One of these housekeepers turned my constant reading into a lifelong love of stories and a refuge from a difficult world. When I came home from school, she would tell me wonderful, exotic stories that are still with me. I discovered, after she left, that no one could take my books away from me and I could always escape into a story.

When my mother was hospitalized and my father felt he could not keep up with all the demands of work and parenting, we moved in with his brother and sister-in-law on Long Island. We remained there for about a year after my mother died. My mother, like her mother, died shortly before her thirtieth birthday, also leaving a son and a daughter. Like my mother, I was just short of nine years old. I was convinced that I too would die before my thirtieth birthday. I was less sure about the two children part.

Insight: *I developed ritualized, repetitive patterns as a mechanism for coping with change. Remembering this has kept me from falling back into that habit. I also discovered potential roots of racist attitudes that would need work later. Finally, I was forced to look at my conflicting attitudes about marriage and family.*

By the time I was nine (when we moved into my aunt's house) I had become increasingly insecure about myself. That self-confident leader from my Hatboro days was shaken by the changes that were going on and, with no one to talk to about any of this, I began to assume that it was all my fault. That there was something wrong with me. That no one really cared about me and it was because of some flaw within me. Maybe it was my fault that my mother was so sick. This insecurity still comes back, no matter how I've worked on it, no matter how successful I've been. It seems that some of us need constant reminders.

Decades later I discovered that there's something called reflected self-concept. Some people only see themselves in what they see reflected by others – bad or good, true or false. They have no internal grounding. I work with clients who have exactly this issue and find myself sucked in and reliving my own trauma while we work on theirs, so each session becomes a reminder. I've read that by age five our personalities are set, so I feel like at least I have a sound base to fall back on, but it takes a lot of work and constant attention to separate out lingering false beliefs from reality.

My aunt's house was the center of her family and the center of the neighborhood. The fathers weren't around much. My uncle was working and getting his engineering degree at night and my father was still living in New Jersey during the week. The house was always full of children – my two cousins, my brother and me, my aunt's sister's children, and seemingly every kid in a four-block radius. Whenever

I could get away with it, I took refuge in the garage, where our old furniture was stored, and read in peace. Although my aunt was very social, I was not. She was sure that I was just stubborn and could fit in with the other kids.

After we moved in with my aunt, this got worse. Everyone else had two parents at home; my father was only around on weekends, and my mother was in the hospital. Clearly, I was weird. I became weirder when Mom died and I was the only child with only one parent. No one had any idea about how to deal with a grieving child. No one talked to me about my loss, and it seemed that I was expected to just forget about my mother. My aunt hadn't liked Mom and she was constantly verbal about that, letting me know that I was just like her and would never come to any good. This, on reflection, was probably the only way she could express the fact that she hadn't wanted us – or at least me – as an added burden. She loved my brother because he was still a baby but saw me as a nuisance.

Decades later, at my uncle's funeral, I found out that my uncle had insisted that we move in with them. It's only recently that I've also realized that my uncle was the only other introvert in the house. He was a quiet man. He should have been a natural ally for me, but that wasn't possible. He worked full-time and was either in class or studying every night to complete his bachelor's degree. My father simply abdicated. He lived in a boarding house near his job, and when he came home on weekends he mostly wanted to be left alone.

School was both a refuge and another difficult adjustment. Again, we seemed to be learning different things than what I'd learned in my last school. I was the only child not living with her own parents and the only child without a mother. I was the only new kid in a school where the neighborhood kids knew each other from infancy (my brother was about two). I was never part of the neighborhood gang and I wasn't a good fit for my extraverted aunt and cousins. It was all too noisy and busy for me. The few friends I made were also misfits for some reason. I tried to connect with other kids by using my allowance to buy them candy. I remember liking school but have few memories of this time other than my thumb freezing around the handle of my clarinet case because I was always losing my gloves.

My strongest memory is of trying to be alone to read. I craved quiet and a chance to retreat into a fantasy world. My biggest comfort was hiding and reading whenever I could. The other was that Mom, after she died, would visit me at night sometimes and we would hold hands and float over my bed.

I had a whole collection of fairy tales and other books that my grandfather had given to my mother. The heroines in the fairy tales were stubborn and independent. Those in my mother's books were always strong, independent orphan girls who made good and/or rescued their relatives from some plight. I modeled myself after these girls, and it's been a sub-theme for many of my career choices. I always was counter-authoritarian. I always preferred the underdog. Lots of mothers told their daughters that it was just as easy to marry a rich man as a poor man. My coaches told me that it was just as easy to coach rich clients as poor ones. I wasn't buying it.

At home, I always seemed to be in trouble. No one knew how to deal with a grieving child except by urging the kind of frenetic activity that went against my introverted, daydreaming grain. No one talked about these things. I'm not at all sure that adults thought that kids had feelings. I was constantly angry and frustrated. I remember reading a poem about an angry girl who went outside and kicked a tree. One afternoon, when everyone else went out and I was left home I went out and kicked the closest thing we had to a tree – a fragile rose tree. I didn't realize how fragile it was and I destroyed it. I got the beating of my life.

Insights: *One reason why I became fiercely independent at an early age was that I had no support. I thought that my feeling of being disconnected was my fault and that no one wanted to take care of me.*

In fact, no one knew how to deal with grieving children. They did the best they could. How many assumptions might you be making about your childhood that have affected your adult relationships?

That summer, I was packed off to summer camp, where I learned how to ride and swim and developed an interest in crafts. It was a welcome change and allowed me enough freedom to be more like my old self. It was this YWCA camp where I first became friends with children from other religions, races, and cultures. It was also where I learned a bunch of "Native American" songs that on closer inspection turned out to be Hebrew folk songs.

About a year after we moved in with my aunt, my father came back from a conference in California and announced that he was getting married. I'll never know if it was love or escapism.

They both entered into this relationship based on fantasies, it seems to me. She had a classic MG and he had a sailboat, so they both assumed the other had money. He wanted to have fun and she seemed to be a party girl. She was the only woman in an engineering firm and had always wanted to get married to validate her femininity. He wanted a mother for his two children. Although everything I knew about stepmothers I'd learned in fairy tales, I wanted this woman to love me and tried as hard as I could to earn her acceptance, split between a need for love and feeling disloyal to and missing my mother.

What I didn't realize was that this woman knew nothing about children or parenting and her own mother had raised her to be cold and distant. We were probably doomed from the start. Dad and I flew to California for the wedding and, tucked into a sort of shelf on the back of the MG, I accompanied them on their honeymoon – the drive back to New York. It's understandable that I felt like a third wheel. They had put a cushion on the toolbox behind the seats for me to nest in. I got my first hint at what my stepmother was like at the Grand Canyon. She urged me to stand near the rim of the canyon so that she could take a picture and kept urging me to take just another step back. We picked up my brother and moved to suburban New Jersey.

Shortly before my tenth birthday, I became the built-in babysitter for my brother, and a part-time housekeeper. I remember spending a lot of time polishing my stepmother's copper-bottomed pots. I don't remember much of this period. I don't remember having any friends or doing anything but going to school, coming home, and cleaning.

Within a year, Edith came to hate the East Coast and decided to move back to California. Dad decided we were all going, so we ended up driving back across the country with the MG hitched to the family car. When Edith got angry with me she'd force me to ride in the MG. We settled into the San Fernando Valley. I had never seen anything like my school there! It was a series of pink stucco buildings. I liked school and was more popular than I'd ever been before – being an Easterner made me instantly perceived as smart and sophisticated.

While school got better, things at home got worse. My stepmother was quickly adding physical abuse to verbal abuse. On weekends, most of the time I was charged with taking my brother with me to a neighborhood park. We'd pick up bottles along the roadside to cash in for enough to buy candy. In my one fling at dishonesty, I'd sometimes send my brother to the counter and shoplift. Once I got caught, we were banned from the store, and I carried the guilt with me.

The physical abuse that Edith inflicted had two effects. It made me often hit my brother when he wasn't behaving, mimicking what was happening to me. I felt guilty but couldn't completely stop. Also, I sometimes had marks from Edith's beatings. She would sit on my back and beat me until her arms were tired or tell my father I'd done something wrong and make him hit me with his belt. Her favorite way of getting me up in the morning was to pull on my bangs until I fell out of bed – the upper bunk. This was decades before child abuse was reported, so the adults in charge of programs never reported it, but they did notice and began to treat me differently, and again I felt like it was my fault. No matter how hard I tried to please Edith I never could, and since my father never defended me, what she said about me must have been true.

My stepmother wanted me out of the house and was hoping to find some reason to send me to a reform school, or at least a convent school, but settled for a small local boarding school. Although I missed my father, brother, and new baby sister, I loved this school. I became very close with my English teacher. I idolized her, and she gave me constant positive support. She also taught me how to write. Weekdays were wonderful, but weekends were lonely, because I never went home and my father, torn between me and his wife, didn't visit often. I would ride and help take care of the horses. Later, I became friendly with the daughter of a Hollywood starlet and was swept off for an occasional glamorous weekend with her and her mother.

Soon, though, our housemother became ill and was no longer able to care for us. Her sister, who ran the school, decided that this was my fault and spanked me for it. At the end of the year, Edith and Dad had to find somewhere else for me. Just another layer of guilt and increased certainty that I didn't belong anywhere. My grandparents came for a visit and Edith found the perfect parting gift for them – me. I understood enough to know that she would have done anything to get me out of the house. My father, ever the conflict-averse people-pleaser, didn't seem to object.

Returning to the East Coast to enter eighth grade was a disaster. West Coast transfer students are considered to be behind their East Coast peers, so I was put into the slowest of the eighth grade classes. My teacher admitted to realizing that this was a mistake, but she was so thrilled to have one bright child in her class that she did nothing about the situation.

Going back to New York City was a difficult adjustment. Obviously, I felt, there must be something dreadfully wrong with me if my family didn't want me. It didn't occur to me for decades that Edith had serious problems and that my father was a wimp. This begin to dawn on me when, after my father's death, Edith sent my brother home with our grandparents, and later when my half-sister moved out of Edith's house at fifteen because her mother was by then an alcoholic with alcoholic boyfriends who kept hitting on my half-sister.

Even so, I still was sure that there was something wrong with me. The pattern of achievement and low self-esteem that I developed in high school continued with me through college and for most of my adult life. I always had to be doing more, and I never felt I was doing well enough. I never believed any evidence of my own successes.

Although I was a skinny kid, Edith kept telling me that I was fat. I still can't eat cottage cheese because she made it a staple of my diet. One Christmas, she was so furious that my grandparents had sent me roller skates that she made me stay outside skating all day, excluded me from the family meal, and fed me beets and cottage cheese for Christmas dinner. When I moved in with my grandparents I also moved into puberty and began to put on weight. Dad, who was a little heavy, would keep harping on fat in his letters to me – admonishing me to not get fat, to watch what I ate. Finally, my grandmother got so fed up with this that she started sending him letters talking about how fat he was until he stopped, but the damage was done, and I finally did become a fat kid. Not obese, but bigger than most of the girls. And, of course, I got bullied. It was only one guy, but I can still hear him – "You look good today. (Pause) Who stepped on your face?"

We had social dancing in eighth grade and had to pair off in size place (height). One very thin boy kept trying to dance with me and I kept moving to end up with the one heavy-set boy. It wasn't until years later that I found out that the thin boy had a crush on me. The heavy boy stood me up for our year-end dance. Didn't want to be seen with the fat girl, I guessed.

Insight: *In retrospect, it's easy to see the pattern of negative – and untrue –messages that I was given. Each new layer of negative* *messages reinforces the old layers to a point where you no longer doubt that they are true. As a child, it's not easy – perhaps not possible – to make these distinctions. As an adult, it's time to take a second look, reframe, and take that weight off your shoulders.*

At home, although my grandmother was indulgent, she was also distant. My grandfather's alcoholism was getting more and more out of hand. He was verbally abusive to my grandmother and me, and sometimes physically abusive of her. Although he was loving when he was sober, he was rarely sober for long. I was terrified of him. He never hit me, but he pinned me down on more than one occasion and threatened me sexually. What I'd learned about men and trust and abandonment left me not any too interested in romance.

Since I had returned to the neighborhood where my parents had grown up, I went to the same high school they had attended. I also became very close to my maternal cousins, who were growing up in the house where my mother and her brother had grown up. I loved visiting there. My cousin and I played in the basement playhouse that my grandfather had built for my mother. My uncle had met and married my aunt while he was stationed in Germany. She was beautiful and gracious, and we all imagined that she was a princess from a fairy tale.

My eighth-grade teacher had kept me in the bottom class so that she could have the pleasure of a good student. Because I had been in a lower class in eighth grade, I was tracked into a lower class in high school, and it took me a year to get moved into the honors section – the top two classes. I was luckier than in eighth grade because the principal had fond memories of my father, who had been extraordinarily popular (my mother was always shy), and he looked out for me.

Finally, I was able to take pride in being smart and doing well in school. My father and I now had more to write about. He would tell me stories about my Latin teacher, who hadn't changed since he taught my parents. I became involved in school service and the literary magazine.

I finally made friends when I got moved into the honors section. We were all what would later be classified as nerds and were, for the most part, socially behind for our age. We were in the same classes and sat together at lunch. We were in the same clubs – Arista, band, religious clubs. Few of us were dating; we tended to just hang out in interchangeable groups. We went to all the football and basketball games together. Our social lives centered around Youth Fellowship or CYO (Catholic Youth Organization) on Friday nights. In the summer, the girls all went to Rockaway beach together to work on our tans and go on the rides in Rockaway Playland. We used to beg for the first ride on the roller coaster. It was free. Decades later, I realized that it was actually the safety run and we were taking our lives into our hands.

One challenge was having a great wardrobe. Every semester, my best friend and I had a fifty-dollar clothing allowance. The challenge was to put together as many combinations as possible to never wear the same outfit twice in a two-week period. We got very good at this mix-and-match concept. The challenge was to see how much money we'd have left over. If we did a pretty good job, we'd buy fries and cherry lime rickeys at the bus depot. If we did really well, it was hamburgers and hot fudge sundaes. This wardrobe planning skill still serves me well. I can tell you every piece of clothing I own and what it goes with. I've taken over the management of some friends' closets.

I joined the literary magazine/yearbook staff immediately. We shared a publications office with the newspaper staff and had joint term-end parties. Both of my parents had been on the *Clipper* staff and my father was editor in chief. I loved it. I wrote short stories and very, very bad poetry. We evaluated all submissions and often had to find titles. We knew that it was time to take a break when someone suggested the perennial dreadful title – "Lucky Red Shirt and Sticky Back Pocket." It was a huge disappointment, though, when another girl was appointed as co-editor in chief. I felt like I wasn't good enough.

My desire to become a teacher created a couple of interesting academic non-choices. When it came time to choose a language, we were asked who wanted to be a teacher and everyone who raised their hand was conscripted into Latin. I suppose that three and a half years of Latin and a semester of Greek did improve my vocabulary. Mostly, it proved to be great fun as we created our own group, dubbed the Catalonian Conspiracy. My sort-of boyfriend wrote funny plays mocking our teachers and we had catchphrases that never failed to crack us up.

The second time I foolishly raised my hand I ended up taking Public Speaking. I hated it. I never wanted to have to get up in front of a group and speak. The teacher, Mr. Sheppard, was the voice of the Yankees and was allowed to leave early on game days. He liked to make his teaching life as easy as possible, so if he liked you, you had to take a second semester of Public Speaking. I hated it twice. Still, everything I learned came back to me decades later when I started training City employees.

During mid-term week my freshman year, I went home for lunch between tests to find out that my father had been killed in a car accident. This is the first time I consciously remember using humor to get through a situation. I went back to school to take my second test of the day, but I made my girlfriend tell me every joke she knew to get me through the experience.

Perhaps because I felt like I'd lost him when I was sent to live with my grandparents, I weathered my father's death better than my mother's. I took refuge in school and school activities, and, despite a weight problem, managed to have a boyfriend of sorts. I was an editor of the literary magazine, a class officer, one of the major organizers of our senior variety show, and part of the most active, popular group in the school, but I never realized my own power. I continued to feel like an outsider and guilty about some unspecified dirty secret. Few outsiders ever got past the seeming normality of my grandparents' home to see what really went on.

Insight: *The pattern of combined over-achievement and low self-esteem that I developed early in life continued with me through college and still persists. It is compounded and underscored by similar patterns I had learned from my family. I always had to be doing more and I never felt I was doing well enough. I never believed any evidence of my own successes. No place – except deep in the pages of a book – was really safe. It was important to try to please everyone and stay as close to invisible as possible if you didn't want pain – emotional and sometimes physical. It was important to hide a lot of your life. It was important to stop and observe to figure out how to fit in. What patterns, once recognized, do you want to change or eliminate?*

I kept my home and school lives as separate as possible. I was always afraid that if I invited friends home my grandfather would show up drunk. Because of this and complicated by general low self-esteem and weight issues, I never realized how many friends I had. When I was putting together acts for our senior variety show it came as a huge surprise when popular kids (who I'd been too shy to ask) wanted to be in my acts.

Insight: *Coping with negative beliefs and overcoming difficulties can lead to positive adaptations. Abuse, isolation, and mislabeling led to the strengthening of positives including leadership, creativity, academic success, humor, writing, and organizing. How have you turned negatives into positives?*

When I was ready to go to college, I knew that I couldn't stay home. In those days, the city university had different standards for boys and girls. So, if you were a boy, you could get into any of the city universities with an 85 average, but if you were a girl, you had to have a 90 average. My high school average was 89.5, so even if I had wanted to, I couldn't go to any of the City University Senior Colleges. I could have gone to community college and transferred to senior college but I wasn't doing that; I wanted to get away from home. I applied to Cornell because that's where my parents had gone. My mother never finished but my father finished after World War II and I figured that I was a legacy so they had to take me; they didn't.

The only other school that I applied to was the State University at Albany. I fell in love with it the minute I saw the place. It was brick and ivy colored and just wonderful. It was barely the State University then. It started as a Normal School, then became the State Teachers College at Albany but had sort of just grown up at the time I got there. This was '63 so we were beginning to get political in New York City, but politics hadn't really hit upstate in the same way it hit every place else. There were as many students from New York City and Long Island as from Albany and upstate New York, so it was unusual for there to be a lot of diversity of opinion, people of color other than a handful of foreign students, any openly gay people. We were, for the most part, united in our naivete. There was generally a rift, as there still is within the state, between upstate and downstate.

When I left home to attend the State University at Albany, a whole different world opened up to me. I loved college; I had a double major in English and Comparative Literature and an Education minor at that point, and I was preparing to teach high school English because, after all, I had always loved English and I wrote in high school.

Away from my family, I could be whomever I wanted to be. I had been dieting the summer before and didn't feel too out of place (i.e., fat). I discovered diet pills, and every month one of my closest friends and I would take the bus to the city to get our supply. I managed to remain thin for most of my college years.

I enjoyed my classes and made friends easily on my freshman corridor. We were one of the last entering classes to hold onto traditions established a generation earlier, like freshman camp, class rivalry, and moving up day – each with songs and rituals. We were also quickly becoming increasingly politically aware. In November, tragedy bound us all together as we spent days in front of the TV crying through the coverage of John F. Kennedy's death and funeral. That February we again came together in front of a TV – this time to watch the first American performance by the Beatles. At the end of the year, we raised money to send some of our classmates to the South to register Black voters and we marched on the governor to protest tuition increases.

Most of my college experience continued in this pattern of conflicting interests and experiences. I worked on an underground newsletter yet rushed a sorority. My friends were beatniks and conservatives, Greeks and Independents.

I alternated between sitting at my sorority's table in the main cafeteria and hanging out in the dark, smoke-filled room dubbed the Cave. This is where all the literary types, film geeks, and political types hung out. We missed the beatnik era and were years away from hippies existing so we called ourselves Cave-ites. We dressed in black or brown and created a literary/political publication called *Suppression*. I spent hours typing rexograph stencils – a nightmare form for reproducing. It was nearly impossible to make corrections on these as the typewriter keys made indentations in a sort of ink gel page. You had to carefully smooth out the error, get the page to line up again, then retype – or just start over. We would sit in a corner of the peristyles, an underground passage that connected the academic buildings, and try to sell the copies.

I discovered Dexedrine and was thin and popular with men for the first time in my life. It was great to be noticed for my looks, but I was in no way prepared for the experience. I had a hard time managing a social life. I went out on dates, but I was unable to become deeply involved with anyone. I was unwilling to give up my independence and

I was afraid. Whenever I thought about my mother and grandmother, I was sure that the same fate awaited me – I would get married, have a son and a daughter, and be dead before I was thirty. If that wasn't a sufficient deterrent to intimacy, I was sure that my grandfather would follow through on his sexual threats if he found out that I was in a relationship.

During my freshman year, I had a very intense relationship with a sociology major. My fears surfaced when he told me that he loved me. I insulted him, and he moved on. Unfortunately, I regretted what I'd said, but was never able to change the situation. I continued to make friends with an eclectic group including students from India, Mexico, and Iran and the few African American students on campus. I dated men from the surrounding all-male colleges – Union College and RPI – and from a little farther away, Yale. These men seemed more sophisticated, but they led a strange existence in worlds where women only existed on weekends. I'm still fascinated by the idea of a man who shows up only a couple of days a week. It feeds right into my need to maintain a strong separate existence and the conflict between my desire to establish a meaningful romantic relationship with a man and my fear that I would lose my own identity.

I tried to spend vacations any place but home. I went to summer school and spent breaks with friends whenever possible. When I had to go home, I tried to bring a friend along to act as a sort of buffer. Sometimes, when friends were there, my grandfather drank less or at least confined himself to his bedroom once he was drunk.

I was sure that I'd be a teacher right up until I got to student teaching. I discovered very quickly that I had no sense of discipline or class control and had trouble managing the elite eighth-graders in the campus school. I really had a hard time controlling the class, but I had a wonderful mentor who taught reading, and he got me interested in being a remedial reading teacher.

The main campus was surrounded by Albany High School and the

Dr. Susan R. Meyer

annex to Albany High School. We would walk down the block and very tall teenagers would sort of come up behind us and somehow kick snow over our heads and into our faces. It gave me a clue that maybe high school students would be a bigger challenge than I'd imagined. I graduated and left Albany without any clear idea of what would happen next, buoyed by the naiveté of youth and without a plan.

When I graduated from college, I had no idea what I wanted to be. My student teaching experience left me feeling that, although I was a good, creative teacher, I lacked the skills or maturity to control a class. I had majored in English Education, so my options were limited. I moved in with my grandparents until a friend and I could get jobs and an apartment. My typing skills were not good enough to get me into a publishing company, and the wait for a teaching job was at least a year. There were three other choices for English majors at that time – work for the welfare department, work for the State, or be a reader (i.e., clip articles) for *Time* magazine. I ended up taking a state job as an employment interviewer because it paid $100 more a year.

The job was dull. I was interested in working with the applicants – interviewing and counseling – but very little of that went on. I was in the Apparel Office and most of the applicants were seasonal workers on layoffs from their regular jobs. They didn't want a new job. They just wanted to remain eligible for unemployment insurance. We pretty much rubber-stamped these people and tried to find ways to amuse ourselves. We had to look busy, and we weren't allowed to read anything but *Women's Wear Daily*, so we developed elaborate telephone games (mostly Botticelli – a game where someone would pick a category, and everyone had to find a name for each letter of the alphabet) and spent our downtime working out the answers and phoning each other with the answers.

A close friend and I finally found an apartment in Manhattan, settled into three rooms of cast-off furniture, and learned to fend for ourselves. Even with our salaries (she was earning probably $5,500 as an editorial assistant), we seemed to have more money than we knew what to do with. I remember stashing excess cash in the freezer. We were out most of the time. These were heady times for political activities and the arts. There were art shows on the street in the Village (Greenwich Village). There were Happenings. There was music everywhere. There was a new wave of feminism, and Black political groups were growing, as was the anti-war movement, so there were meetings all the time. I discovered consciousness raising and joined a New York radical feminist group. We seemed to split our time between marching and raising money to support Planned Parenthood and legalized abortion and affirming a woman's right to not have to spend hours making herself beautiful.

We marched in Manhattan. We loaded onto buses for anti-war demonstrations in D.C. and for a counter-inaugural to protest Nixon's election. We staged a feminist protest at MoMA. For many of us, this was slightly less about political protest than the center of our social lives. Most of the protests had a party atmosphere. I still have a picture of a group of us forming a giant multi-ringed circle, huddled together in a field to keep warm during a protest in Washington. We were young and we were having a wonderful time in the name of social justice. While this was a phase for some, it shaped the political perspective and career choices of many. We were going to change the world.

The assassinations of Robert Kennedy and Martin Luther King changed this party environment, and as we moved into our mid-twenties, political activism shifted to the more serious business of focusing on our careers and on supporting political candidates who represented our views. In New York City, that meant Bella Abzug. Her energy drew me in – that gravel voice, those hats, that drive. She represented the power that we knew women should have.

One friend, still politically active in her mid-seventies, chose a career in copy editing because it rarely actively engaged her brain, leaving more energy to support her political activities. She's still actively

Dr. Susan R. Meyer

engaged with her causes today and has used her editorial skills to edit newsletters and books related to those causes. She's another good example of using transferable skills.

Eventually, I couldn't stand my job another day and went back to school. I had become interested in remedial reading as an undergraduate and thought that offered an alternative to teaching in a high school. Unfortunately, the Board of Ed did not hire reading teachers. People were promoted from within for those jobs. I should have done a little research instead of going for the quickest escape.

I lived in Chelsea and had an off-and-on romance with a guy I had met as an undergraduate. While I was getting my master's in Educational Psychology, he was getting his in Student Personnel Administration. He had gotten me a part-time job with the school's catering service – mostly coat check and setting up trays of cookies for parties.

The first thing the permanent staff taught us was how to arrange a single box of cookies so that it would look like two boxes. This meant that we almost always went home with at least one box of cookies. Those cookies, from Sutter's bakery, were a mainstay of our diet for a year. During evenings, my two upstairs neighbors and I sat around listening to music, getting a little high, and eating leftover cookies. I hope to never hear the theme from *2001: A Space Odyssey* again.

When we could afford to, we would have Sunday breakfast at Sutter's – croissants and the *Times* – and listen to the boyfriends and girlfriends of inmates at the House of Detention call up to their lovers. My on-and-off romance continued over the next five years. I was hoping to spark a romance with his former roommate, who, at this time, was still my upstairs neighbor.

After I finished my master's in Educational Psychology/Reading, I once again didn't know what I was going to do for a living. I managed to get a temporary job with a reading program that was being introduced into elementary school. That lasted twelve weeks. Then – I don't remember how – I had the opportunity to sub in a day care center. I enjoyed the work and eventually found an assistant teacher's position in Greenwich Village. My colleagues as well as the parents were almost all hippies. It was a very mellow existence with children named Apache and Moonbeam and mothers who designed tie-dyed shirts or clothing made from dishcloths. I enjoyed working with young children, loved the minimal structure, and this fit my lifestyle perfectly. For a while, I was very happy not being in charge of anything.

I moved on to become a head teacher at another day care center by this time and had also moved out of Manhattan to an apartment just off the King's Highway train station in Brooklyn. My sort-of boyfriend and his (unbeknownst to me boyfriend) roommate warned me that this was a bad move, and that spending all my time with my close friend and her family would make me pretty much a social isolate. This repeats the old introvert-social butterfly dichotomy from my childhood.

The new center had an emphasis on mental health, and I became increasingly involved with children with emotional problems. I also started a reading readiness program. With an Iranian assistant and a Cuban aide, I had an international team supplemented by volunteers and mental health workers. I enjoyed my day care experience, and it gave me the opportunity to nurture many children who needed me. At the same time, I took an active role in parenting my goddaughter. These activities allowed me to fulfill my maternal needs.

Eventually, though, I became much more interested in the needs of the parents. I managed to have my staff working so efficiently that I could spend most of my time out in the hall with parents, but I was growing out of the job. Somewhere in this time period it became clear that my boyfriend and I both wanted to date the same guy – my upstairs neighbor. The two of them are still living happily together.

I knew that I didn't want to stay in day care, and I knew that I wanted to do something that involved teaching and counseling adults, but I didn't know exactly what that would look like, so I did something I was very good at – I went back to school. Unfortunately, I didn't think much about how I was going to pay the bills. I was able to eke out an existence with a student loan and unemployment.

I had subbed for a few days in the public schools. It reinforced what I felt about my classroom management skills when I had finished my student teaching. I hated it so much that I took my phone off the hook every morning for the rest of the year. About this time, a good friend in my second master's program – this time in counseling – invited me to join him at a taping of *$20,000 Pyramid*. I was invited to try out to become a contestant, and just at the point where I was considering bankruptcy as an option, I was selected for the show. Twenty-nine seconds after the game began, I was $10,000 richer.

By this time, I recognized a pattern in my life – I was the Queen of the eleventh-hour comeback. I had learned to rely on myself by the time I was eight. By the time I was twenty-one, I had broadened that out to trust in the universe. No matter how bad things got, if I kept my mind open, did everything I could think of to do to aid the process, and believed that everything would be okay, everything always was.

Of course, I also found out quickly that meditation and reliance on God was not going to be enough if I didn't do my part. I have a vivid memory of deciding to repaint my kitchen while preparing dinner for friends. I was calm and serene – I could get everything done. God would provide. Well, neither one of us turned on the oven, so my guests, faced with a raw chicken, had a vegetarian evening!

I also began to learn that how you view yourself in terms of success and failure should come from within yourself. The problem, of course, is that many of us tend to measure ourselves by our peers. And, sometimes, we have a real overachieving group of peers. One of my fellow interns at the counseling center was a wonderful woman with excellent counseling skills. Her only problem was that she saw herself as no one. She never felt that she was as good as her husband and friends.

This was a hard one. Her husband had been part of a former president's cabinet. Her two closest women friends were successful professionals. One of them had just signed the biggest book deal on record. The other was the internationally known media figure Barbara Walters. Tough competition! It took a lot of work to help my friend recognize that she had chosen a different – lower profile – field and was brilliant at what she did and every bit as successful in her own right. This is something I'm still working on today.

When I was a counseling intern, I helped establish the new Counseling Center. I enjoyed the process of getting something new going. It drew on the same skills that I had used to successfully transform my day care classroom. There were four part-time counselors on staff. As interns, we met weekly with our advisor to discuss our progress and to discuss the interactions among the group members. At the last session, we were all asked to talk about the things that we felt were important – had gone well. I spoke about the camaraderie among the group and how pleased I was that we could all confide in each other and were supportive of each other. I was shocked when one of my peers said, but Susan, we all come to YOU! It was like getting a standing ovation. It's a good example of my lack of recognition of my own strengths.

Insight: *Many of my choices that appeared to be random or unconnected were part of a pattern of continuous experimentation and approximations that would eventually lead me to my true path. There were lessons learned in each step of the journey, even though I didn't realize this at the time. I think this is often true for many people.*

I've always felt a strong pull between theory and practice and have spent most of my career trying to successfully integrate the two. Although I enjoy a good theory and really like synthesizing diverse information to generate theories of my own, I have no patience for something that can't be put into – or at least connected to – practice. I needed to find settings where I could use my theoretical background to make something happen.

When I outgrew day care I had no firm career plans except to find a position that involved counseling adults. I lived off my *Pyramid* winnings for a year, but eventually had to find something to do. I tried to find a college counseling opening but didn't have any luck. One of my problems was that I had no confidence. Another problem was that I managed to telegraph my feelings if I wasn't really excited about a job. This left me pretty much unable to sell my skills in any interview.

Eventually I realized that a third problem was that, with seven years in day care, I was having a hard time getting anyone to believe that I could work with adults. I would need some kind of transitional job to build my credibility as someone with experience with adults. The only job I could find was with an employment agency. This job involved managing the payroll for the temp division. I have always been terrible with numbers, and while I liked the environment, I lived in terror that I would make some monumental error and none of the temps would get paid. I couldn't take the pressure and finally quit, believing that I was about to be offered a counseling position at a SUNY college.

Unfortunately, there was no reality to that dream, and I ended up working for another agency, this time soliciting openings and making placements. I hated it. I was no good at selling. I hated the impossibility of placing clients who didn't have the "corporate crisp" look that was expected. I hated that the other placement counselors would make fun of applicants who didn't live up to their standards of appearance. Although I was excellent with the applicants (using my career counseling skills), I rarely got job listings.

This was a base salary plus commission job. Because I wasn't making placements, I wasn't getting commission checks. The base salary was $150 a week, just about enough to barely cover my expenses. I didn't have the appropriate clothing. The wardrobe coordination skills that I'd developed in high school enabled me to dress appropriately on a very limited budget. The cooking skills that were pretty much in my blood enabled me to stretch a pound of spaghetti with homemade meat sauce (ground beef was still cheap) into a week's worth of dinners when I was really broke. For the price of a Happy Hour drink, we loaded up on free bar food as often as possible.

In the meantime, I was building credibility as someone who worked with adults. After a few months, a woman who was to become a close friend joined the staff. She immediately began badgering me to leave, telling me repeatedly that I was in the wrong field and encouraging me to resume my job search. I'm eternally grateful to her.

Exactly one year after I had taken my first employment agency job, I found a position as a Cooperative Education coordinator within the City University of New York. They needed someone with counseling skills and a knowledge of the secretarial field. A year of placing office personnel plus my master's degree made me the perfect candidate.

I had given up my Chelsea apartment and moved to Brooklyn, first in a semi-communal relationship with an old college friend, her former fiancé (now a gay activist), his teenaged sister, two dogs, around five cats, and a white rat, then to a place of my own.

I spent the next seven years working in the Cooperative Education Program at Medgar Evers, a primarily Black CUNY college. When I started, the average student age was twenty-six and the population was overwhelmingly female. I loved the students. It was a little strange being a minority faculty member – one of a handful of whites. It was also difficult at times to find a niche at the college as someone perceived as an administrator in a sea of academics and as a grant-funded employee rather than on a college line. These distinctions brought out other biases and issues around status. My own experiences at the college made it easier for me to help my students learn to succeed in work environments where race, age, education, and status were often issues.

Counseling had fulfilled my need to help people. My interest in the field, however, was limited to practical concerns. I was most interested

Dr. Susan R. Meyer

in how counseling could be used as a teaching tool. It was in Co-op that I was finally able to blend all my skills – teaching, counseling, job placement.

At the college, I developed a career planning course that focused on life histories and discovered many unforgettable women. About the time I became increasingly fascinated with life histories, I decided that, if I was going to establish myself in academia, I needed my doctorate. I knew that I would never return to NYU, so I investigated Teachers College, Columbia. I really knew nothing about the field of adult education, but I reasoned that at least the population would always be around. As I looked at the program more closely, I realized that it was the perfect field to bring together my interests in counseling and teaching.

Although I never considered myself a political activist, I have strongly held opinions and beliefs and try to create an environment that supports them. When I was working on my doctorate, a new non-traditional doctoral program was in its infancy. There was a big emphasis on the new program, and I was one of a handful of students who felt that the traditional doctoral program was getting short shrift. One other woman and I brought a diverse group of students together to form a tightly knit lobbying group. We brought our concerns to the department and were able to bring the traditional students back from second-class status. We pushed one professor to read our papers himself instead of giving them to a graduate assistant, arranged a departmental reception, registered for courses previously reserved for the non-traditional students, and got the faculty more involved in our progress.

During this time, I helped two of my professors initiate a new professional organization – the International League for Social Commitment in Adult Education. We felt that there was no venue for continuing the strong tradition of service and social action in many adult education programs. Figures like Eduard C. Lindeman, and Myles Horton and Paolo Freire, all pioneers in adult learning, had established a tradition that was becoming lost in an increasing emphasis on preparing for the professoriate and an increasing emphasis on staff development and training. This conference provided a voice for the activists and helped a wider range of adult educators to examine the principles underlying their practice. It gave me the opportunity to work closely with people I idolized.

Insight: *I rarely acknowledged my leadership and organizing abilities, going all the way back to high school. I discovered how often I had been a leader when I wrote my life history. What skills have you downplayed? Why?*

Many of these same people would be influences in later parts of my adult education career. The experience I gained through this conference enabled me to work with a professor at Teachers College, Columbia to create an annual conference focusing on workplace learning. It also allowed me to become involved in planning a conference on transformative learning and be a small part of working to develop a theory of transformative learning.

I was working very hard, juggling a full-time job and full-time graduate study. I didn't have any time left for more of a social life than a quick coffee before class. As the pressure to finish my dissertation before my fortieth birthday and before grant funding for the Co-op program ran out, I was barely speaking to even my closest friends. David's Cookies was my new best friend!

In every job I have had, I have tried to do my best. I have worked to improve things. I'm driven to be successful at whatever I do, and to be perceived as knowledgeable and a leader, although I don't necessarily want this for the power – more for the recognition and for people coming to me for assistance.

When I was in day care, I knew nothing about early childhood when I started the job. I spent the first year absorbing everything I could

Dr. Susan R. Meyer

from good teachers. When I got my own classroom, I began to explore how to improve things. I get easily bored when things stay the same for too long, so I'm always looking for ways to innovate. My favorite group was old fours and young fives – it's a wonderful age, because they're becoming articulate, and you can almost see them developing opinions about the world.

My classroom became the focus for mental health activities at the Center. I was given most of the children with problems because I could handle them. I developed a reading readiness program patterned after Sylvia Ashton Warner's. Every day after lunch, we would spend a little time at the lunch table reviewing the children's vocabulary. Each child had cards with words on them. These were words that were important to that child. If they didn't learn the word, it was unimportant and therefore discarded and replaced with a new word. When a child had enough words, he or she could make simple stories out of them.

My classroom ran very smoothly. My assistant, aide, and I were a close-knit team, and we played off each other's strengths. My room ran so smoothly that I was able to spend more time outside the room counseling parents or inside the room spending more time with special needs children.

At the college, I became totally immersed in my work. I revised the curriculum for the four Co-op placement courses and became involved in the departmental curriculum committee, established to set up a uniform career development curriculum across programs. I established a career library. I designed a workshop to train faculty coordinators.

When the grant money finally ran out, I had to leave the college. I tried to make the transition to independent consultant but didn't have the marketing skills or confidence to get work. I looked for another college counseling position but was unwilling to leave New York because I didn't want to leave my family and friends. Finally, when I was running out of money and ideas, I remembered that a former student of mine, who worked in the Mayor's Office, had told me to give him a call if I was ever looking for work. This was seven years later, but I needed another eleventh hour miracle, so I called him. Within days I had a new job at HRA's Office of Staff Development and Training.

At HRA, I had to hit the ground running. I had a brand-new doctorate in Adult Education, but no idea what HRA was about and, other than the one workshop, no experience with staff development. At least my teaching in the Co-op program was very similar to training. I was lucky to be working with two managers who were generous teachers. I was immediately immersed in AIDS Awareness training. AIDS was just coming to the forefront as an issue for welfare clients. It was taking a toll on people who might be classified as traditional welfare recipients – IV drug users, etc.

AIDS created a whole new group requiring services. Many new applicants were middle- to upper-middle-class men. Before they became ill, they had held a much higher standard of living than most recipients. The rents that they could no longer pay were far higher; the medical care they needed much greater and more expensive. These were also people who were unfamiliar with the Income Maintenance bureaucracy and often too weak to cope with it. There were also problems with fear and misinformation among staff assigned to clients with AIDS.

We needed to immediately launch into a massive education campaign for personnel who had no information about the disease and little compassion for the clients. I helped develop an executive overview for the commissioner's direct reports. This was the beginning of two years of AIDS Awareness training. I helped develop a train the trainer program and trained 150 trainers in AIDS Awareness. I also designed, supervised, and participated in training for line staff, including all the employees in the City's homeless shelters.

I was not in this job very long before one of the women I reported to left and the other retired. By this time, I was supervising three other trainers, all of whom were social workers with many more years of experience in training than I had. When my manager retired, I was given most of her responsibilities and now had seven people reporting to me. I continued to be involved in special projects, including designing new caseworker training for the Division of Adult Services.

During this time, I also developed a trainer development program and worked with several hundred trainers to improve their skills. It was through these classes that I was recruited for my next job. One of the women I trained felt that I would be a good person to have at the new Child Welfare academy, a new training unit devoted solely to the preparation of children's protective services workers. I was offered and accepted the position of Director of Trainer Development.

This was a wonderful opportunity for me to bring together a variety of skills. I was working developmentally with the staff that I would be seeing over a long period of time. This meant that I could help each of them add to their skill base at an individualized pace, rather than just a one-shot approach.

I began to work closely with the curriculum development group as well and had a chance to concentrate more on reflective learning. As we tested out each new curriculum, I worked with the authors to ensure that the material matched the learning intent and that the learner was provided with a developmental path. At the same time, of course, this process further developed the abilities of the trainers and developers. Although I loved my colleagues and the strong sense of dedication and camaraderie, I hated the commute. As the staff became too busy to attend my programs, I grew bored and began seeking new challenges.

My next move was again into a totally new area. I accepted a position supervising a Defensive Driving program with the Citywide Department of Personnel's Office of Staff Development and Training (OSDT). I knew nothing about Defensive Driving, but I wanted the opportunity to supervise staff again. Also, I liked the idea of starting up something new and I was promised the opportunity to expand the job.

What I didn't like was feeling like an outsider – Defensive Driving was regarded as a second-rate program by staff members who worked with the professional development courses. I felt that I had to prove myself. I became involved in the annual needs assessment and in program evaluation. This led to setting up an Evaluation Forum and developing Trainer Development courses. I also started to become involved in the professional development courses. When we decided to implement a new format with certificate programs combining core managerial and supervisory courses and electives, I was part of the development team. I was asked to design a mentoring program for participants in the managerial certificate program. During the next two years, this program expanded from fifty participants to 150 and expanded to include managers mentoring supervisors. I had expanded the trainer development series to thirteen courses, including distance learning courses. I became involved in citywide reengineering projects.

I was also teaching at Teachers College and becoming involved in a new venture there. I was invited to help create a Workplace Learning Institute, a program that would bring students, scholars, and practitioners together to examine issues in the workplace. This was an exciting and productive period where I was able to use all my skills in one position. Unfortunately, the mayor did not see training as all that important. Our programs were about to be cut drastically when my supervisor accepted a new position and asked me to come along as her deputy.

This change became another uphill battle – a theme in my career. Once again, I was the outsider – this time in an organization that believed strongly in promoting people up through the ranks. It took almost four years, but, finally, I was able to carve my own niche as the expert on mentoring and on management development programs.

During this time, I also developed a trainer development program and worked with several hundred trainers to improve their skills. It was through these classes that I was recruited for my next job. One of the women I trained felt that I would be a good person to have at the new Child Welfare Academy, a new training unit devoted solely to the preparation of children's protective services workers. I was offered the position of director of Trainer Development.

I'd had a hard time adjusting to OSDT for many reasons. The first was that, because of how I'd gotten the job, people were nervous around me, thinking that I had special protection from the Mayor's Office. Second, I wasn't a social worker. I hadn't come to this office with field experience. Third, I was younger than the people I was supervising. While I was proud of my work, I didn't think that anyone else necessarily thought I was doing such a great job. I was surprised, then, when I was given the office's first non-retirement farewell party. The pattern continued.

At the Child Welfare Academy, I was director of Trainer Development. This was a wonderful opportunity for me to bring together a variety of skills. I was working developmentally with the staff I would be seeing over a long period of time. This meant that I could help each of them add to their skill base at an individualized pace, rather than just a one-shot approach.

I began to work closely with the curriculum development group as well and had a chance to concentrate more on reflective learning. As we tested out each new curriculum, I worked with the authors to ensure that the material matched the learning intent and that the learner was provided with a developmental path. At the same time, of course, this process further developed the abilities of the trainers and developers. Although I loved my colleagues and the strong sense of dedication and camaraderie that they had with each other, I was, once again, the outsider. I hated the commute. As the staff became too busy to attend my programs, I grew bored and began seeking new challenges.

Insight: *When assignments are varied and each involves both new learning and building on existing skills, it can feel like you have a serial career without actually leaving a single employer.*

In the first chapter, I talked about patterns that develop in childhood that stay with us throughout life. Some of my most negative circled back all too often. Therapy and coaching have helped me recognize them when they crop up and I've developed some pretty good coping mechanisms, but sometimes nothing seemed to help. When this happens, it's time to deal head-on with fear. Much of what you'll find here is a tale of avoiding that fear or taking temporary measures. It becomes clear, though, that while temporary fixes may let you get back to some level of function, it isn't until you are ready for the pain of facing your fears that you can become fully the person you are meant to be.

What I've learned is that postponing the hard work means making the same mistake over and over again. If you want to stop being a people pleaser – if you want to stop believing all that bad press you're writing about yourself – you can't avoid the deep thinking, the search for what's really true, and the reframing that lets you move on. I see clients early in their careers who are in jobs that are eating them alive. "I'll wait a few more months to see if I get that promotion," they say. "It's not so bad," they say. We look at the fears that are keeping them stuck. Some are brave and begin the hard work. Some aren't yet ready – and even the best coach in the universe can't create that readiness – and will live in the pain that they know instead of looking at the pain that is stopping them. If you are on the fence, it's time to jump. It doesn't have to be a big jump or a deep dive. Start with gently stirring the waters or taking a tiny hop and see how that feels.

Early Warning Signs

I spent a lot of time in my mid-twenties shaping my life around pleasing mostly fictitious men by proving how strong and independent I was to guys who were no longer in my life. I would envision them reemerging and, upon discovering how strong and independent I was, proposing to me so we could go off to happily-ever-after-ville. I'd go to the supermarket thinking, M_ will be so impressed that I can carry my own groceries, totally ignoring the fact that a) most people can manage to carry their groceries and b) M_ was happily touring Europe with his wife. I had an amazing interior life. It almost compensated for the gaps in my real life.

For quite a while, this was enough. I was mostly carefree and just a little lonely. I was happy enough working as an assistant teacher in Greenwich Village. Theater and movies were cheap and there were enough political/protest activities to keep everyone busy and surrounded by like-thinking people all the time. The thing was, at the end of the day I was still alone and unhappy. I didn't realize that I was depressed until, while on a walk with my preschool group, I stopped dead in the middle of the street. I was frozen in place. Another teacher had to physically prod me into motion.

That scared me enough to send me straight to a therapist. It didn't take long for me to realize that I knew more about counseling than he did, but he did help me surface some of my core issues and get back to functioning better. As I reflect on this, I'm sure that I chose him because he was safe and not sufficiently skilled to get me to really face my issues. I wanted a Band-Aid, not surgery.

Through most of my adult life I didn't feel good enough. I would prove myself again and again, but, even when I was getting accolades for my work, for my cooking, for my leadership, it never seemed real. Off and on I'd found someone to shore me up when I needed help. Often, this was short term. Not the best solution, but it was something. A quick fix might be better than a glass of wine at the end of the day, but it may not last much longer and it doesn't make that baggage you're carrying any lighter. I didn't think about this until all that baggage crashed down around me.

Insight: *Deal with fear as soon as it arises.*

There came a time that I found myself on a roller coaster so fast that I couldn't catch my breath. I was at the peak of my career. I had a solid consulting practice. I developed and managed the first internal coaching program within a City agency. I was teaching coaching at NYU. I had time and money to travel. I had good friends, although they were mostly scattered across the country.

I had gone to an event commemorating the life of my favorite professor and dissertation sponsor and had a conversation with a former student. When I was praising him for his accomplishments, he told me that it was because – looking me straight in the eye – he was standing on the shoulders of giants. Wow. I was floating. Soon after this, he asked me to join the faculty of the Columbia Coaching Certificate Program. This was a dream come true.

I knew that Teachers College needed to have a coaching program. Both doctoral programs in our department had transformative learning as a major focus – what better home for coaching? I had pushed for the program. I finally got one of my fellow coaches to push my former student to start thinking about this and, while interdepartmental politics kept me off the program's faculty, I followed its growth closely. Finally! I would be part of this.

You may have noticed that all this good stuff does not include success in my personal life. This is where you can see how the parts of your life that are not in great shape and the baggage that keeps them the way they are will, at some point, come back to bite you. Big-time.

I felt great about my life – didn't even miss being in a relationship. I didn't, after all, need anyone. In fact, I saw this as a positive shift from trying to please a fictitious life partner. Then, everything came unraveled. The city got a new mayor, who hired new commissioners, who instantly tore down all the programs that their predecessors put in place. That meant the end of my contract with New York City's Human Resources Administration (HRA) – my biggest client. My Buddhist group broke up, ending what had become a strong spiritual connection and source of support.

I was depressed. I thought that I should have been able to do something to save the program. My income disappeared. I no longer had a City contract, so I didn't have that as a source of future employment. I was pretty much broke. There was a lot of shuffling at NYU, and I didn't get any new classes. I got turned down for unemployment because I had a website, therefore a potential source of income.

But I still had my dream spot teaching in the Columbia Coaching Certificate Program. My dream quickly turned into a nightmare as I discovered that as much as I loved the program I simply wasn't a good fit. It required being structured – and I'm not a structured person. It required teaching in a way that was antithetical to all that I see as my teaching strengths. It didn't help that I hadn't had enough time to really digest the program in it's entirety before being thrown in, and that because the program was quarterly there was too much time between repetitions. It also didn't help that I wasn't assigned a mentor and was expected to somehow know everything that was in the curriculum.

The biggest issue, though, was that I was trying too hard to be someone I wasn't. It reminded me of when I worked for employment agencies. It was important to look, dress, and act a certain way that they called "corporate crisp." I did my best, but it wasn't me. I remember a guy at a party laughing when I told him that I was dressed in my best corporate crisp. His response? "You couldn't be corporate crisp no matter how hard you tried." Same thing. I couldn't get the rhythm. The language, the style. Instead of thinking that this simply wasn't me, though, I took it as a failure that I couldn't remold myself. I was disappointing my former student and I was disappointing myself. I had to resign.

So, clearly, all of this was my fault, and I was a total failure. Just to re-inforce this, during the time I was teaching in the Columbia Program I took on a new coaching client. Pretty much everyone I knew had turned down working with this agency. A fellow coach, who worked with them in a different capacity, and couldn't also manage this, thought I might be able to help the agency. Of course, my Superwoman mindset kicked right in and I accepted the contract. Huge mistake.

While the Executive Team proclaimed their desire for open, authentic communication, what they actually wanted, individually, was to never share anything but everyone else would share with them and allow them to comment. That was the least of their problems. Instead of seeing the experience as a losing battle, I took it as a personal failure. This and the Columbia failure overlapped. Clearly, I was stupid and worthless. I hadn't tried hard enough.

I was drifting into depression before I lost the HRA contract. I just didn't realize it. I was gaining weight, sleeping a lot, avoiding people, not doing anything. At first, I thought it was just aging. I was, after all, past sixty-five. Then I decided it was medical, since anemia, thyroid medication, diabetes, and blood pressure medications all contributed to depression. It was time to see if an antidepressant would help – almost all of my friends had been on them for years.

I tried a low-level antidepressant that never made me feel better. It turned out to be most often used with cancer patients to increase their appetite as much as to improve their mood. Not the best choice for someone already eating anything in sight. I discovered that a friend had the same experience. She'd buy a cake to have dessert for the week, then pick up a second one "just in case," then go home and eat both of them. We both opted out of that med pretty quickly.

For a couple of months, I did nothing. I sat at home. I watched really bad television. I overate. I didn't shower any too often. When I finally couldn't stand the way I looked or smelled I decided to do something about it. I went back to my old coach for a while and I started coaching myself. I took a couple of amazingly healing writing workshops.

Insight: *Create and maintain an early warning system for yourself*

.

If you ignore every warning sign and wait until you bottom out, it can take years to repair and heal. If you catch yourself before you start to isolate...or stop showering...or substitute chocolate for people...you can reclaim your life.

It wasn't quick and it wasn't easy. I ditched the antidepressant. I joined a gym to have access to a treadmill. I ate less and better. I forced myself to get out of the house and spend time with other people. I reconnected with friends I'd ignored for a long time. I took a long, hard look at what I wanted for this next phase of my life and created a new set of goals and an action plan

Dr. Susan R. Meyer

Chapter 9

Exercises

Sometimes, you want to find a specific exercise and also don't want to be hunting through an entire book to find it. This chapter contains all the exercises in the book organized by chapter. Some are repeated in more than one chapter and those will appear here only once – in the first chapter where they appear.

The Strategies:

1. Explore your life.

Take time to document your roots as well as your work history. This will help you identify your values, your strengths, and your potential obstacles or stumbling blocks and to see how these may be rooted in your family history. The information will help you make more informed choices.

2. Know your skills and challenges.

Whether you do a full analysis or make a list, knowing what you can – and like to – do helps you expand your thinking beyond work similar to what you've already done and to explore new possibilities. It also helps you identify things that you find difficult so that you can clearly identify potential trade-offs or compromises.

3. Maintain and expand relationships.

We all need a strong support network. Identify yours. Periodically check and update your family and friendship circles.

4. Recombine skills.

There are so any different ways to use your skills! A consultant who went from working with people with substance abuse issues to young entrepreneurs was not surprised that both groups relied on the same core skills. Think about skill clusters before you focus on specific jobs. Look at how your skills fit together in unexpected ways.

5. Be patient; experiment and stay open to miracles and new possibilities.

Experiment; tell everyone what you're looking for and ask a lot of questions. Expect the unusual. Say yes more often. Be surprised!

6. Deal with fear.

This doesn't mean putting yourself in danger. It means stretching. It means not holding back out of fear of failure. There are good outcomes to be had from mistakes.

7. Reassess; reprioritize.

Over time, your skill set changes. Some are so rusty from disuse that you may never bring them back to their original luster. A few have become obsolete. Some that you once loved you may never want to use again. Examine what may be holding you back.

The Exercises

Chapter 1: Exploring Your Roots

Creating a Life History

Life history serves as a jumping-off point for self-understanding and self-acceptance as the path to fulfillment. Using the format here, you can flag major events and influences. The mileposts and patterns will serve as the basis for the detailed analysis.

Since this is a voyage of exploration, there are very few rules. There are a few things that you probably will want to at least consider in reviewing your life. If some of these topics don't apply to you, ignore them. If some are painful, try to come back to them. If you absolutely can't write about any of these areas, try to ask yourself why and record your response.

This is not therapy, and it is not sharing. Everything here is for you alone. Although I will share with you some ways to organize the information about your life, I don't know each of you personally, so I would not presume to interpret.

Family

- What do you remember about your grandparents? Were they (or other older relatives) a significant factor in how you were raised? Did they shape your values or role expectations?
- Describe your parents. How did they spend their time? How were you raised?
- What are some significant incidents that give a clear picture of how you related to your parents?
- Who was in your immediate circle when you were growing up? Was it just the nuclear family (mom, dad, kids, pets) or did you have an extended family (grandparents or other adults in the house, cousins or other relatives so nearby that you were almost always together)?

- How did this influence your values or attitudes? How did you relate to/interact with these people?

Childhood Markers, School

- What were some of the marker events, or most significant incidents in your childhood?
- What kind of school did you go to? How did you do in school? How did you feel about school?
- What were your favorites? What did you dislike? What were your successes? Your failures?
- Did you go on to higher education? Why or why not?
- If you did go to college, describe your college experiences. Who was important to you? What were your successes? Your failures? Did – how did – college shape your post-school decisions?

Work

Answer these questions to include all degree and advanced training programs.

- Where did you live when you finished school?
- Why? How old were you? What were your plans?
- What is the first thing you remember wanting to do when you grew up? If this changed, when and how? If you could be that thing now, would you?
- Describe your work history. Don't forget to include work inside the home. Yes, raising a family counts! You used countless skills to do this.

For each work experience – paid or unpaid, full- or part-time – describe how you felt about the work. Describe how you felt about yourself as a worker.

Relationships

Chronicle your social life.

- Who are your friends?
- How long have they been friends?

- What links you to them? How do you spend your time together?
- Describe your romantic life. Who has been important to you? Why? How long did each relationship last? Did you marry or make a long-term commitment to another person?

Leisure

- How do you spend your free time? What kinds of activities do you enjoy?
- Are they individual or group activities?
- Are you involved in any sports? Active in a gym? Take yoga or other classes?
- What artistic activities do you engage in?
- What are your creative outlets?

Spirit

- What is your religious background?
- Were you actively involved in religious activities as a child?
- Has this changed in adulthood?
- Do you still practice your faith of origin, or have you switched or stopped?
- How do you satisfy your spiritual needs? Formally or informally? Alone or with others?

This list is a starting point. Write as much as you can, then go back and write some more. If you are over thirty, you should have the equivalent of at least twenty typed pages – more than twice that number in a handwritten document.

Analyze Your Life History
Identify Your Successes

- Start reading through your life history. Read slowly and carefully to identify and mark your successes. Mark them all. Add additional successes that occur to you as you do this.

- Until you see it written down, you may have no idea of all the things that you have done well, all the obstacles you have overcome, all the people you have influenced. Now is the time for you – finally – to be impressed with yourself.

- As you read each incident that makes up your life history, concentrate on the evidence of success. If, as you read, you realize that you have glossed over an event, write more. Once you've identified your successes, you'll be looking at how you felt at the time.

Feelings About Success

Review each success to identify the emotions related to the experience to link your feelings to your achievements Now, go back over every success that you marked and answer the following questions:

How was I feeling about myself at the beginning of this experience?

Your purpose here is to learn from your successes so that you can repeat them. Your emotional state, whether you realize it or not, had some influence on the actions you took.

Emotions can't be separated from action. Intuitively, we understand the importance of context and of emotions in understanding our actions.

If you have lost touch with your emotional context, this is a good time to begin flexing those intuitive muscles. Reclaim your emotions and understand exactly how they work for you. This is a big part of owning – being fully in touch with – all aspects of your own life. Recognize that no one ever operates in a vacuum. You are part of a universe rich in hopes, dreams, fantasies, and feelings as well as actions. Which of these have guided you to make the right choice?

If I was experiencing negative emotions, what did I do to use them in a positive way OR what did I do to work through them or get beyond them?

Dr. Susan R. Meyer

Were you afraid? What did that feel like? How clearly can you identify your fear? In what ways did being afraid stop or limit your actions? Did you make choices based on what was safest? Were you unable to make a choice? How long did that last? If you worked through your fear, how were you able to do this? Did you develop a technique that you were able to transfer to other situations?

If I was experiencing a positive emotion, what was it? How did I use it?

What did success feel like? How do you use those feelings as motivation in other situations?

Past Influences

Review each success to identify how you achieved your successes.

How did I plan for this? What in my life prepared me for this experience?

Even the most serendipitous events in our lives can reveal some prior preparation. Connecting to the skills and experiences that have prepared you for a challenge helps you become clearer about what is at your disposal as you move to new challenges in the future. Marcia Sinetar, author of *To Build the Life You Want, Create the Work You Love*, identified a group she calls Creative Adapters; people who "don't simply adjust, they improvise with superior figuring-out skills." You are identifying your own skills in creative adaptation in this exercise.

What did I do well?

Sometimes, you are the last person to recognize your own strengths. This phenomenon is something we have often seen when working with organizations. People in organizations make extraordinary things happen every day but are often oblivious to their own success. "We got lucky," they say. "Somehow it just worked out." Don't believe this for a second! If you talk to these people long enough about how it "just happened," you can begin to tease out the thought, the skills, the prior practice that led to the right decisions at the right time.

You need to be able to do the analysis that tells you exactly why you succeeded every bit as much as organizations do. The problem in the workplace is that if the individuals that make up an organization are going to learn and grow – and repeat their successes – they have to understand what they did right. So do you. You have to understand the pattern of your successes. You need to know what you drew on from your prior experience at this moment so that next time you are faced with a challenge you can do the same thing. How can you repeat a positive behavior if you don't know what it is?

What events in my past helped me understand this situation? What skills did I develop in other areas that I was able to transfer to this situation?

Have you developed skills that you were able to rely on because you had this experience before, or did you generalize and transfer skills from other – seemingly unrelated – experiences? Are there events in your past that made you avoid certain options or choices? Did your past experience serve you well or did it prevent you from selecting the best plan of action as quickly as you might have wanted?

Identify Challenges

Identify all the rough spots in your life to learn how you have handled challenges.

How was I feeling about this experience?

Some people see hardships or problems as challenges or opportunities. Others see them as insurmountable obstacles.

What was I imagining could happen? Were my worst fears realized?

There are two reasons for writing down your worst fears. One is that sometimes just seeing them in writing restores a sense of perspective. The second reason is that, for many people, this is a crucial step in remembering what planning was done to meet the challenge.

It may be that at the time you actually did engage in a little catastrophizing. Where did that lead? Were you paralyzed or did you move on? Sometimes, dealing with worst-case scenarios helps spur creativity and leads to new – unexpected – courses of action.

How was I feeling about myself during this experience? Did I feel in control or out of control?

We spoke earlier about identifying emotions. Sense of control is related to but may be slightly different than fear and anxiety, so it is important to look at it separately. We see this same theme of letting go of control in Buddhism, in Gestalt therapy, and in existentialism – the notion of living in the moment. How often have you done this? How comfortable were you?

What did I do to resolve the situation? What did I do for myself to cope?

Everyone reacts differently in what they perceive to be a crisis. Some have spent so much time creating contingency plans for every imaginable situation in life that they need only select the appropriate one and proceed. Others take the ostrich route: hide, do nothing, and wait for the crisis to blow over. A third group, true pessimists, or fatalists (or both) to the end, simply remain passive, neither hiding nor taking action. They predict that the outcome will be bad and feel that nothing can be done to change it. They wait until the crisis has passed, shrug, and pick up the pieces – if there are any – and start over.

Then there are those whose lives seem to be one big crisis. One group is the perpetually problem laden. Their lives never run smoothly, but they never see any of their problems as of their own making. They do have one special talent, however; they can always find someone to sort things out for them. People flock to these people's sides to solve their problems. Of course, these people also have a gift for making their helpers feel genuinely appreciative. They are grateful for all assistance and often reciprocate in every way that they can.

A second group mirrors the fatalists discussed earlier. They know that their lives will be a series of chaotic situations. They are not by nature planners, nor are they pessimists. They ride out every crisis, usually taking random actions without evaluating the impact of these actions. Sometimes everything works out wonderfully well; sometimes it's a bust. These people rarely know why.

A third group thrives on chaos. They expect that all change requires a certain amount of confusion and feel that life is a nugget of gold, shaped by fire, and blows into something beautiful. Their confidence helps them get through crises.

Which type are you? Are you a whole other type? Does your crisis mode move you forward or hold you back?

Who helped me? How? Did I ask for help or was it offered?

We rarely succeed in a vacuum, but we sometimes do not understand our own pattern for seeking help. Some acknowledge the support of their friends at every turn; others may not realize just how much support they have had. This is a good place to do a quick inventory. You will be looking at two things at once. First, you will be creating a list of your supporters. This list will be organized into categories elsewhere, but as you create the list, you should begin to look for patterns. Do you rely on a wide circle of supporters or just a few? Do you rely on certain people for only one kind of help? Second, try to remember how you felt about actually asking for help.

Influences on My Life

Review each success to identify the people who helped you along the way to remind yourself of who your friends are.

Who influenced you? Who have you influenced? Who are all the people you have touched in your life? How did you influence them?

We often think that we go through life unnoticed. We think that we have not contributed anything to the greater good. It is easy to fall into a depression and feel useless. This exercise will remind you of just how much of an influence you are. Make the list as long as you can.

As we move through our own life, we touch so many others' lives, yet we rarely are aware of the impact we have on others. Use your life history as a resource for this list. Work with two columns here so that, as names occur to you (or descriptions if the names are gone) you can add them to either side. Some names may belong on both sides of the list.

Chapter 2: Know What You Know

These exercises will help you get a clear picture of your skills, strength, and potential obstacles. They also provide a framework for planning your career.

Life History or Skills List

Document every skill and talent you have. You can write a detailed life history that will give you some insight into your development over time, your reaction to unfortunate experiences, and the environments in which you thrived. I constructed a chronological life history for this book, describing in some detail not only every job I've had but also the general environment, grounding the work in time. I thought I'd captured everything and had the experiences in the correct sequence until I unearthed some old resumes and discovered some work experiences I'd totally forgotten. I learned some new things about myself in the process.

Although knowing yourself is more complete if you write your full life history, at a bare minimum you can learn a lot by creating a detailed skills list. Reflect on your life and create a master list of all your skills. This can range from baking great cookies through being the star of your soccer team to advanced computer skills. Make the list as long as you can. Include every experience that added skills – jobs, volunteering, clubs, extracurricular activities, sports, hobbies, and home/family responsibilities. Now, go back and add specific skills for each experience. Don't leave anything out. For example, do you cook? That involves reading, shopping, knowing prices, planning the components of the meal, understanding nutrition, weighing and measuring – at a minimum. Be thorough.

Identify Your Successes

Start reading through your life history. Read slowly and carefully to identify and mark your successes. Mark them all. Add additional successes that occur to you as you do this.

Until you see it written down, you may have no idea of all the things that you have done well, all the obstacles you have overcome, all the people you have influenced. Now is the time for you – finally – to be impressed with yourself.

As you read each incident that makes up your life history, concentrate on the evidence of success. If, as you read, you realize that you have glossed over an event, write more. Once you've identified your successes, you'll be looking at how you felt at the time.

Feelings About Success

Review each success to identify the emotions related to the experience to link your feelings to your achievements. While usually success makes us feel good about ourselves and about the world, sometimes success leaves us feeling vulnerable either that we're in over our heads and will be found out to be a fraud or that something horrible will happen and our success will collapse.

Now, go back over every success that you marked and answer the following questions:

How was I feeling about myself at the beginning of this experience?

Your purpose here is to learn from your successes so that you can repeat them. Your emotional state, whether you realize it or not, had some influence on the actions you took.

Emotions can't be separated from action. Intuitively, we understand the importance of context and of emotions in understanding our actions.

If you have lost touch with your emotional context, this is a good time to begin flexing those intuitive muscles. Reclaim your emotions and understand exactly how they work for you. This is a big part of owning – being fully in touch with – all aspects of your own life. Recognize that no one ever operates in a vacuum. You are part of a universe rich in hopes, dreams, fantasies, and feelings as well as actions. Which of these have guided you to make the right choice?

If I was experiencing negative emotions, what did I do to use them in a positive way OR what did I do to work through them or get beyond them?

Were you afraid? What did that feel like? How clearly can you identify your fear? In what ways did being afraid stop or limit your actions? Did you make choices based on what was safest? Were you unable to make a choice? How long did that last? If you worked through your fear, how were you able to do this? Did you develop a technique that you were able to transfer to other situations?

If I was experiencing a positive emotion, what was it? How did I use it?

What did success feel like? How do you use those feelings as motivation in other situations?

Past Influences

Review each success to identify how you achieved your successes.

How did I plan for this? What in my life prepared me for this experience?

Even the most serendipitous events in our lives can reveal some prior preparation. Connecting to the skills and experiences that have prepared you for a challenge helps you become clearer about what is at your disposal as you move to new challenges in the future. Marcia

Sinetar, author of *To Build the Life You Want, Create the Work You Love*, identified a group she calls Creative Adapters; people who "don't simply adjust, they improvise with superior figuring-out skills." You are identifying your own skills in creative adaptation in this exercise.

What did I do well?

Sometimes, you are the last person to recognize your own strengths. This phenomenon is something we have often seen when working with organizations. People in organizations make extraordinary things happen every day but are often oblivious to their own success. "We got lucky," they say. "Somehow it just worked out." Don't believe this for a second! If you talk to these people long enough about how it "just happened," you can begin to tease out the thought, the skills, the prior practice that led to the right decisions at the right time.

You need to be able to do the analysis that tells you exactly why you succeeded every bit as much as organizations do. The problem in the workplace is that if the individuals that make up an organization are going to learn and grow – and repeat their successes – they have to understand what they did right. So do you. You have to understand the pattern of your successes. You need to know what you drew on from your prior experience at this moment so that next time you are faced with a challenge you can do the same thing. How can you repeat a positive behavior if you don't know what it is?

What events in my past helped me understand this situation? What skills did I develop in other areas that I was able to transfer to this situation?

Have you developed skills that you were able to rely on because you had this experience before, or did you generalize and transfer skills from other – seemingly unrelated - experiences? Are there events in your past that made you avoid certain options or choices? Did your past experience serve you well or did it prevent you from selecting the best plan of action as quickly as you might have wanted?

Identify Challenges

Identify all the rough spots in your life to learn how you have handled challenges.

How was I feeling about this experience?

Some people see hardships or problems as challenges or opportunities. Others see them as insurmountable obstacles.

What was I imagining could happen? Were my worst fears realized?

There are two reasons for writing down your worst fears. One is that sometimes just seeing them in writing restores a sense of perspective. The second reason is that, for many people, this is a crucial step in remembering what planning was done to meet the challenge.

It may be that at the time you actually did engage in a little catastrophizing. Where did that lead? Were you paralyzed or did you move on? Sometimes, dealing with worst-case scenarios helps spur creativity and leads to new – unexpected – courses of action.

How was I feeling about myself during this experience? Did I feel in control or out of control?

We spoke earlier about identifying emotions. Sense of control is related to but may be slightly different than fear and anxiety, so it is important to look at it separately. We see this same theme of letting go of control in Buddhism, in Gestalt therapy, and in existentialism – the notion of living in the moment. How often have you done this? How comfortable were you?

What did I do to resolve the situation? What did I do for myself to cope?

Everyone reacts differently in what they perceive to be a crisis. Some have spent so much time creating contingency plans for every imaginable situation in life that they need only select the appropriate one and proceed. Others take the ostrich route: hide, do nothing, and wait for the crisis to blow over. A third group, true pessimists or fatalists (or both) to the end, simply remain passive, neither hiding nor taking action. They predict that the outcome will be bad and feel that nothing can be done to change it. They wait until the crisis has passed, shrug, and pick up the pieces – if there are any – and start over.

Then there are those whose lives seem to be one big crisis. One group is the perpetually problem-laden. Their lives never run smoothly, but they never see any of their problems as of their own making. They do have one special talent, however; they can always find someone to sort things out for them. People flock to these people's sides to solve their problems. Of course, these people also have a gift for making their helpers feel genuinely appreciative. They are grateful for all assistance and often reciprocate in every way that they can.

A second group mirrors the fatalists discussed earlier. They know that their lives will be a series of chaotic situations. They are not by nature planners, nor are they pessimists. They ride out every crisis, usually taking random actions without evaluating the impact of these actions. Sometimes everything works our wonderfully well; sometimes it's a bust. These people rarely know why.

A third group thrives on chaos. They expect that all change requires a certain amount of confusion and feel that life is a nugget of gold, shaped by fire, and blows into something beautiful. Their confidence helps them get through crises.

Which type are you? Are you a whole other type? Does your crisis mode move you forward or hold you back?

Who helped me? How? Did I ask for help or was it offered?

We rarely succeed in a vacuum, but we sometimes do not understand our own pattern for seeking help. Some acknowledge the support of their friends at every turn; others may not realize just how much support they have had. This is a good place to do a quick inventory. You will be looking at two things at once.

First, you will be creating a list of your supporters. This list will be organized into categories elsewhere, but as you create the list, you should begin to look for patterns. Do you rely on a wide circle of supporters or just a few? Do you rely on certain people for only one kind of help? Second, try to remember how you felt about actually asking for help.

Influences on Your Life

Review each success to identify the people who helped you along the way to remind yourself of who your friends are.

Who influenced you? Who have you influenced? Who are all the people you have touched in your life? How did you influence them?

We often think that we go through life unnoticed. We think that we have not contributed anything to the greater good. It is easy to fall into a depression and feel useless. This exercise will remind you of just how much of an influence you are. Make the list as long as you can.

As we move through our own life, we touch so many others' lives, yet we rarely are aware of the impact we have on others. Use your life history as a resource for this list. Work with two columns here so that, as names occur to you (or descriptions if the names are gone) you can add them to either side. Some names may belong on both sides of the list.

Reflect on Your Career Decisions

Reflect on the career decisions you've made so far. Why did you make each choice? Did you actually make a choice or just go with the flow somehow? Look for patterns or connective threads. Why? Because it helps to know both how you got where you are and where you are going.

Skills Analysis

After you have listed all of your skills, go back and assign weights to each skill in terms of level of use, level of ability, and level of enjoyment.

How high is your level of ability?

    5 – I'm great at this

    4 – I'm better than most

    3 – I'm just about average

    2 – This is really not one of my best things

    1 – Are you sure you want to let me touch this?

How often do you use this skill?

    5 – About as often as I breathe

    4 – Most of my time centers around this

    3 – Maybe half the time or a little less

    2 – Often enough to remember how to use it

    1 – What skill was that?

How much do you enjoy using this skill?

    5 – I would probably pay to be able to do this

    4 – Few things in life make me happier

    3 – Take it or leave it

    2 – Maybe someone else would like to give it a try?

    1 –It sets my teeth on edge

Here's an example of weighted skills:

Skill	Level	Use	Enjoy
podcasting	4	2	4
creating new programs	3	4	2
presentation skills	5	1	5
develop mentoring programs	3	3	2

Create a second list that contains all your potential challenges. This will help you develop a skills grid.

Skills Categories

When you have finished, you will be able to divide your skills into four categories:

    Display shelf – skills to be used most

    Building blocks – skills or behaviors that can be developed

                                      Dr. Susan R. Meyer

Recycle – skills or behaviors that can be used differently

Goodwill/trash heap – skills or behaviors that we want to throw away

List four to six skills in each category.

Display shelf	Building Blocks
Recycle	Trash Heap

Update this grid on a regular basis – at least annually. When you're ready to explore new possibilities, look for jobs or experiences that rely on your display shelf skills, supported by building block skills. Avoid Recycle and Trash Heap skills. Evaluate what's in each quadrant in terms of your list of challenges. Decide what, if any, trade-offs you are willing to make.

Summary of my skills and challenges through college:

Skills and Assets	Potential Obstacles
Solid Foundation	Learned to stay in the background
Resilience	Loss of trust
Working with children	Low self-esteem
Creativity	Poor self-image
Writing	Needing external validation
Typing and filing	Poor typing skills
Wardrobe planning/coordination	Weight issues
Public speaking ability	Hate public speaking

Each time you are evaluating a career choice, review these two charts. One of the best pieces of career advice I ever got was that it is just as important to know what you don't want as it is to know what you want. What are you passionate about? Are you willing to deal with an obstacle to do what you love?

For example, I'm willing to deal with public speaking because I love to teach and do workshops. I'm willing to type in order to write books or create curriculum yet will never again type as a core job responsibility. Know your trade-offs. Know how and when you are willing to use your non-preferred (storeroom) skills (and for how long) in order to make a dream come true. Review your trade-offs periodically.

Know Your Values

There are three areas to look at as you think about potential career choices. We've talked about identifying potential challenges and organizing your skills. Another filter that will improve the quality of your choices is understanding your values. After all, your values define who you are. They also inform every choice you make – especially your career choices. Not only are you looking for work that reflects your core values but also work that does not honor those values.

You might not choose a position that required such long work hours that you could no longer spend time with your children or participate in meetings or leisure activities. If animal rights are high on your values list it would not be easy for you to work for an organization that experiments on animals. The interplay of these three factors will enhance your exploration and your choices.

Values List

How will your core values influence your career choices?

Select your top 10–15 values. Use this list as a start and add others as you wish.

Achievement	Helping others	Purity
Advancement	Honesty	Quality of endeavors
Adventure	Independence	Quality of relationships
Affection	Influence	Recognition
Arts	Inner harmony	Religion
Challenging problems	Integrity	Responsibility/ accountability
Change/variety	Intellectual status	Safety

Community	Job tranquility	Security
Competence	Joy	Self-respect
Cooperation	Knowledge	Serenity
Country	Leadership	Sophistication
Creativity	Location	Stability
Decisiveness	Loyalty	Supervising others
Democracy	Market position	Time freedom
Ecological awareness	Meaningful work	Truth
Economic security	Merit	Wealth
Effectiveness	Money	Wisdom
Ethical practice	Nature	Work under pressure
Excellence	Order/calm/conformity	Work with others
Excitement	Peace	Working alone
Expertise	Personal growth	
Fame	Physical challenge	
Family	Pleasure	
Fast-paced work	Power/Authority	
Financial gain	Privacy	
Freedom	Professionalism	
Fullest life/up to potential	Public service	

Write Your Eulogy

One way to begin to see what's important in your life is to look ahead to the end of your years. To do this, you are about to write your own eulogy. This may sound morbid, but it really isn't. The purpose of this exercise is to craft a personal vision.

Organizations do this all the time. They hire expensive consultants to lead them in future searches or "blue skying" because they know that they can't grow or change unless they know where they want to be – the organizational vision. Just as for organizations, when you as an individual understand that vision – what you hope to achieve during the course of your life – your life goals will become clear to you.

Imagine that you are writing your own eulogy. If you find the idea of writing a eulogy upsetting or threatening, picture yourself writing a testimonial being given about you at a big awards banquet honoring your lifetime achievements. Find a quiet, private space and something to write on. Turn off the television. Get rid of any distractions. Take a few deep breaths. Clear your mind of other concerns. If you wish, close your eyes.

Imagine a room full of people who love you who have come together to celebrate your life. Imagine that you have accomplished everything that you ever hoped to do. Your every dream has been fulfilled. Everyone who is important to you is gathered to talk about the wonderful person you were and about your many accomplishments. If you listen, you can hear the speakers. Write down what they are saying about you.

What are all the things you have accomplished? Have you traveled? Where? What have you created? Have you written or painted or played the flute or knitted or gardened? Did you cook for friends? Volunteer at a soup kitchen? Teach someone something? Send perfect postcards or birthday cards?

Write as quickly as you can and don't censor your writing. When you have written as much as you can, put it aside overnight. Now go back to your eulogy and read it very slowly. What did you leave out? Make any additions you feel are important.

Vision Statement

Your personal vision statement should describe what you ultimately envision the greater purpose of your life to be, in terms of growth, values, contributions to society, etc. As you grow and change, your vision and mission may also change. Self-reflection is a vital activity if you want to develop a meaningful vision.

Once you have defined your vision, you can begin to develop strategies for moving toward that vision. Part of this includes the development of a mission statement. What do you want for the rest of your life? Take a few minutes to write down your personal vision, This will be based on your goals and values.

Mission Statement

Vision statements and mission statements are very different. Your mission statement is the vision translated into written form. It is a concrete expression of how you will bring your vision to life. A mission statement should be a short and concise statement of goals and priorities.

Your mission statement should be a concise statement of strategy, and it should fit with your vision. The mission should answer three questions:

1. *What will I do?* This question should be answered in terms of what are the concrete and psychological needs that you want to fulfill.
2. *How will I do it?* This question captures the more technical elements.
3. *For whom will I do it?* The answer to this question is also vital, as it will help you focus your efforts.

Goals

What do you now see as the overall goal of your life? This is generally called an overarching goal. Think of this overarching goal as your mental picture of your career/life trajectory. It's helpful to review your goals periodically to eliminate those that are either completed or no longer relevant and to add new ones.

Write down the biggest current goal you can think of – a real stretch goal – something that will definitely expand your comfort zone. This is your overarching goal, not dissimilar from your personal mission statement, simply a bit more refined – more specific. Then, you will become even more specific as you plan out your sub-goals that support the overarching goal.

Perhaps the simplest way to bring your goal from general to specific is to use a proven goal-setting formula: S-M-A-R-T goals. Check your goal against the S-M-A-R-T criteria and tweak away until it's as clear and strong as possible. When you design a home, if you don't have a really good sense of what the completed building looks like, it will be hard to plan the individual rooms. The criteria are described below.

Specific – as detailed as possible

Measurable – criteria that will indicate progress toward and completion of the goal

Achievable – Is this something that you can actually do?

Realistic – Can this actually happen?

Timely/Time-framed – How long will this take? Is this the right goal for right now?

If you choose to write a full life history, here are some additional exercises to help you develop a deeper look at yourself:

Chapter 3: Stuck Spots

Who's in Your Support Network?

Create and maintain your support circle. This is a four-square model. Put two different names in each box. You'll want to so you aren't over-relying on one person. Also, the names in each box should be different so that you are not asking the same person to play too many roles.

Everyone needs *cheerleaders*. These are the people who applaud you for getting your shoes on the right feet. They provide unconditional support for everything that you do. They make you feel brilliant and invincible. You need them for those days when you're convinced that you are useless, talentless, and totally incapable.

Comforters provide totally non-judgmental support. They will listen for hours and agree with everything you say. They show up with wine and chocolate and a full box of tissues. They bundle you up in a quilt and listen and listen and listen. They stay until they know you are soothed.

Critics help you think things through and find potential flaws in your plans. They do this in a loving way, helping you to find better solutions or create foolproof plans or take your writing from so-so to outstanding.

Confronters call you on your crap. They ask you what you've done about the things you've said you'd do. They are the ones that ensure that you don't hide behind excuses and actually get things done.

These are the people who help you get through life. They're the ones who help you make hard decisions and recover from disasters and take care of yourself and rise to greatness. You'll want a second chart, by the way, that shows you who you support. Refresh your charts twice a year to be sure that the people you have in place are still part of your life in the same way.

Cheerleaders	Comforters
Critics	Confronters

Your support network will be right there to help you if life becomes too overwhelming and you need more help than they can give. They'll help you research your options, evaluate your choices, and make sure that you show up for your appointments.

Vision Meditation

Take five minutes each day to envision the life you want for yourself. Create, in your mind, a detailed picture of how you are living this ideal life. Be very specific. See yourself in that life. Don't think about how you'll achieve this; focus on what it looks like, feels like. Getting caught up in the "hows" limits you. Seeing the big picture opens up possibilities and creates opportunities for synchronicity.

Widen Your Vision of What's Out There

If you keep your eyes open to what you're looking for it will appear. Maybe not quite as you'd envisioned it, but it will be there. An old exercise suggests looking for a red car. Once you see the first one, they will be popping up all over the place. This applies to opportunities as well. If I hadn't followed up on an invitation to a taping of *Pyramid*, I would never have won enough money to live on for a year.

Chapter 4: Trying a Stable Job with a Good Pension

What skills have you learned since you made your original list?

Are there skills that need to be deleted because of disuse (you can't remember how to do them), changes in how the skill is done that you haven't kept up with, or obsolescence (we don't use carbon paper or adding machines anymore)?

Update Your Skills Sort

Over time, the skills on this chart are likely to change. You may now appreciate skills that are currently in your Trash Heap. New skills may have replaced those on your Display Shelf.

Recombine

For this exercise, you'll want to enlist the help of two or three friends. Using your Skills Sort chart, pick a set of four skills. Brainstorm to create a list of every possible career that would utilize those skills. Be creative. Don't allow any limitations. Repeat with a second set of skills. Try for a third. Now, select careers that might interest you. Brainstorm how to move into them. Do some research about them, including looking at online hiring sites to see how each skill is described. Set up some informational interviews to learn more about how to move into the field.

Chapter 5: Tracking Your Life Purpose

Update Your Skills List

What skills have you learned since you made the original list?

Are there skills that need to be deleted because of disuse (you can't remember how to do them), changes in how the skill is done that you haven't kept up with, or obsolescence (we don't use carbon paper or adding machines anymore)?

Update Your Skills Sort

Over time, the skills on this chart are likely to change. You may now appreciate skills that are currently in your Trash Heap. New skills may have replaced those on your Display Shelf.

Recombine

For this exercise, you'll want to enlist the help of two or three friends. Using your Skills Sort chart, pick a set of four skills. Brainstorm to create a list of every possible career that would utilize those skills. Be creative. Don't allow any limitations. Repeat with a second set of skills. Try for a third. Now, select careers that might interest you. Brainstorm how to move into them. Do some research about them, including looking at online hiring sites to see how each skill is described. Set up some informational interviews to learn more about how to move into the field.

Chapter 6: Overcoming Fear and Depression
Rollercoaster Times

Rewrite Your Eulogy or Testimonial

If you have your original visioning exercise, have it handy for comparison but avoid reading it before you complete the exercise. You'll be comparing them. Imagine that you are writing your own eulogy. If you find the idea of writing a eulogy upsetting or threatening, picture yourself writing a testimonial being given about you at a big awards banquet honoring your lifetime achievements. Find a quiet, private space and something to write on. Turn off the television. Get rid of any distractions. Take a few deep breaths. Clear your mind of other concerns. If you wish, close your eyes.

Imagine a room full of people who love you who have come together to celebrate your life. Imagine that you have accomplished everything that you ever hoped to do. Your every dream has been fulfilled. Everyone who is important to you is gathered to talk about the wonderful person you were and about your many accomplishments. If you listen, you can hear the speakers. Write down what they are saying about you.

What are all the things you have accomplished? Have you traveled? Where? What have you created? Have you written or painted or played the flute or knitted or gardened? Did you cook for friends? Volunteer at a soup kitchen? Teach someone something? Send perfect postcards or birthday cards? Write as quickly as you can and don't censor your writing. When you have written as much as you can, put it aside overnight. Now go back to your eulogy and read it very slowly. What did you leave out? Make any additions you feel are important.

Update Your Goals

Go back over your eulogy and highlight your accomplishments, then create a separate list of these accomplishments. What will you need to do to make all of the things that you heard a reality? Those accomplishments you have yet to achieve represent potential goals. They will serve as the basis for planning your life goals.

Review Your Values

Go back one more time and highlight the things people said about you. Look at these in relation to your accomplishments and generate a list of things that you value or that represent your values (e.g. family ties, hard work, friendship).

This exercise will help you create an overall guide for your life.

Revisit Your Personal Vision and Mission Statement

Your personal vision statement should describe what you ultimately envision the greater purpose of your life to be, in terms of growth, values, contributions to society, etc. As you grow and change, your vision and mission may also change. Self-reflection is a vital activity if you want to develop a meaningful vision.

Once you have defined your vision, you can begin to develop strategies for moving toward that vision. Part of this includes the development of a mission statement. What do you want for the rest of your life? Take a few minutes to write down your personal vision. This will be based on your goals and values.

Mission Statement

Vision statements and mission statements are very different. Your mission statement is the vision translated into written form. It is a concrete expression of how you will bring your vision to life. A mission statement should be a short and concise statement of goals and priorities.

Your mission statement should be a concise statement of strategy, and it should fit with your vision. The mission should answer three questions:

What will I do? This question should be answered in terms of what are the concrete and psychological needs that you want to fulfill.

How will I do it? This question captures the more technical elements.

For whom will I do it? The answer to this question is also vital, as it will help you focus your efforts.

Review Your Goals

What do you now see as the overall goal of your life? This is generally called an overarching goal. It's an end point. Think of this overarching goal as your mental picture of your career/life trajectory. It's helpful to review your goals periodically to eliminate those that are either completed or no longer relevant and to add new ones.

Review Your Support Circle

Regularly review your support circle. You may be surprised at how long some people have been in your circle or may find that you barely remember a name or two. Take a moment to thank those few for all they've done before you delete their names and add new ones.

These are the people who help you get through life. They're the ones who help you make hard decisions and recover from disasters and take care of yourself and rise to greatness. You'll want a second chart, by the way, that shows you who you support. Refresh your charts twice a year to be sure that the people you have in place are still part of your life in the same way. Your support network will be right there to help you if life becomes too overwhelming and you need more help than they can give. They'll help you research your options, evaluate your choices, and make sure that you show up for your appointments.

Catastrophize

This is a "what if" exercise that relieves anxiety. By the time you finish it, you may be laughing at your problem or will at least have some possible courses of action.

Imagine the worst-case scenario of an issue that is depressing you or keeping you up at night. Write it down. Then, answer the questions.

Issue: Example – I might lose my job.

1. On a scale of 1 – 10, how likely is that to happen?

2. If it does happen, what will you do?

Based on what you've said you'll do, answer the same two questions. Repeat this five to seven times. How do you feel about the final answer?

Obsessing Break

Sometimes, we can't get a situation out of our mind. This is a technique an actor I know would use when he was waiting to hear about an audition. He had a habit of rubbing his hands on his thighs when he was anxious and was wearing through his jeans, something he could ill afford. He started creating obsession breaks. He would set his timer for five minutes and allow himself to obsess about his situation. When the times went off, he would force himself to move on to something else. I find that this works best if, when the timer goes off, you have a change of location or dive into some chore you've been avoiding.

Puff Balls

When you are feeling depressed or dealing with an old fear or pain, this can be useful. This works best if you can do it with a friend.

Describe the situation that is upsetting you. Go into detail. Find something odd about the story. Expand on that. Can you find something strange or silly in the story? For example, threats of sexual abuse are in no way comical, yet I used this technique to deal with one. As I told the story, I began to realize that the threat was repeatedly worded in a way that somehow sounded chivalrous. With each retelling, it became more exaggerated. With the help of my friend, a fellow coach, I was able to turn the situation into a puff ball. I pictured myself blowing the puff ball away. It's been ten years since I last felt the impact of those threats.

Lists

Sometimes, we need concrete visual reminders of the impact we've had. This is especially useful when you're having an "I'm nobody" moment or when you're feeling alone or unloved.

Make two lists. One will be all your accomplishments with evidence. The second will be all the people who like or admire you, also with evidence. Keep them someplace where you can see them whenever you need reassurance.

Finally, there are excellent coaches, counselors, therapists, and psychiatrists out there. Never be ashamed to get professional help. Always use reputable referral sources and have an introductory session.

Reality Check

People act differently on intentions based on how important the intention is to them. Do a quick check to be sure that this intention is important to you. Is it a distraction? What do you *really* want to do?

You mentioned that you want to work on _____. What have you done so far? Has that been hard or easy? What are you *not* doing?

How have you tried to get going? Is that working for you? Why not?

Clearing Conflicting Thoughts

Everything that happens is a collaboration between you and the universe. Intentions are energy.

All of our intentions are prone to being sabotaged by conflicting intentions, especially the intentions that are really meaningful to us.

Restate your intention. Then outline, in no more than five steps, how you plan to achieve that intention. Are you acting on this plan or stuck?

Sit with your plan for a while. Examine each step by asking the following questions:

- *What's really going on here?*
- *What story am I telling myself?*
- *Is that true?*
- *What evidence do I have to support that?*

If you find evidence to support your story, perhaps this is the wrong intention, or perhaps the story is based on faulty interpretations. Now ask:

- *Where does my story come from?*
- *What might be a reframe or an alternate explanation?*

Chapter 7: Reemerging - Retirement Redefined

Dream/Brainstorm

Go back to your skills chart. Pick two skills from your Display Shelf. Imagine that everything is possible (because, in fact, it is). Create a list of every possible way you can use those skills – every possible job or volunteer experience. Great brainstorming involves doing something called breaking set.

Most lists will begin with fairly obvious choices. You'll want to get beyond those, though. Keep listing possibilities until you get to some that sound ridiculous. Add those to your list! You have now broken set – moved beyond the known into the unknown.

Earlier, I described a woman who thought that she was going to be a teacher's aide and ended up being elected to the state assembly. Break point for her was, in considering alternate careers that used her skills, coming up with circus clown. This got her thinking about public-facing careers and entering politics.

Research

Pick your top three or four new possibilities to research. The research has three parts.

- *Explore the field.* What, exactly, does work in this field look like? Where can you do this? What does it pay? Can you find stories about people who do this work? What has the most appeal for you? Are there tradeoffs or drawbacks? After doing the research, does this still appeal to you? If yes, put it on the short list for Part 2. If no, does your research suggest new possibilities? If yes, explore them. If no, move on to Part 2.

- *Explore getting experience.* Research ways to try out your top contenders. There are internships. There are volunteer experiences. There are work-cations that give you a short-term opportunity to try out something new.
- *Plan.* Check your time and finances. Know how many experiments you can create for yourself.

Experiment and Document

Go for it! Document each experience as you move through it. This will help you know whether this transition is one you want now or want to consider for the future. It may also open up ideas about related fields or aspects of this field that you have not previously considered.

Chapter 10

Final Thoughts

L ife isn't simple anymore. Or linear. Perhaps it never was. When I was in my Counseling Psychology program in the late '70s, a professor told us that the average person entering the labor market was likely to move through at least eleven different kinds of job. We thought this was preposterous. Now, it's true for an ever-increasing number of people.

While there are still some relatively stable fields, they aren't as stable as they used to be. The Social Security Administration opened in 1935. The majority of employees stayed until retirement. In the 1980s there was a mass exodus as nearly everyone reached full retirement age at the same time. That's simply not likely to ever happen again. Civil service, once secure for life, has experience cutbacks and layoffs. Entire agencies have disappeared. Similarly, because of technology and offshore outsourcing, whole careers have disappeared. Switchboard operators have disappeared. File clerks and elevator operators are increasingly rare. If you've called any kind of helpline recently you've run into an answer bot, and if you get an actual human, it's less likely that they're local – or even in this country.This has created an ever-increasing number of serial careerists. Some will have a succession of experiences working for others. Some will start their own businesses – possibly many times over. Some will bounce back and forth between the employee and entrepreneur states. Some will create a successful path of ever-increasing fulfillment. Maybe one of them, whether by choice or by chance, is you. Don't be someone who never finds your true path.

To successfully negotiate a unique career path you will need to be resourceful, optimistic, and ingenious much of the time and always resilient. This book, up to this point, has been about giving you tools and examples. In this chapter, we'll focus on attitude and state of being. At the end, there are some resources that I've found useful for me and for my clients.

Optimism and Courage

This is an extension of the work you've done on visioning with the addition of action. That's where the courage comes in. What have you always wanted to do? If now is the time to assume that it's possible, then create an action plan.

Rebecca had been a highly successful, in-demand IT consultant when her sister developed a fatal brain tumor. Rebecca quit her job to be with her sister until she died. At that point, she felt completely drained and incapable to return to the high-paced consulting world. She wanted peace. She loved the water and had some basic boating skills. She decided that she would be an excellent ship's captain, so she signed up for training and got her license. She moved to Florida. Because she didn't want to be around a lot of people, she created a career moving other people's boats from one port to another. I got a note from her a few years later letting me know how valuable this interlude had been and that she'd rebuilt her IT consulting business.

Courage means not letting other people make your decisions or pass you over or limit you in any way. Push back! One woman I interviewed refused to be pushed out of her position as head buyer for the menswear department in a major department store just because she was a pregnant woman. She was doing an excellent job and she knew it. Another decided that she could sell HVAC systems without knowing anything about them – not even knowing how to write up a sale. Not taking no for an answer led to a multimillion-dollar business.

Resilience

One thing all serial careerists have in common is the ability to bounce back. It takes resilience to move from one career to another, to break through barriers, to make the non-traditional choice. Rebecca is one of a handful of women who became ship's captain. When the television network Sarah worked for turned her down in favor of a man for a foreign correspondent spot, she moved to another network and hosted her own syndicated show.

Resilience involves not taking no for an answer. It involves creating your own options, generating new solutions or work-arounds, and not settling for less than you want and deserve. It also means surviving cancer or a double lung transplant and returning to or creating a vibrant career. It involves spending a lot of time asking "Why not?" instead of "Why?"

Motivation and Morale

Finally, if you don't think highly of yourself no one else will. I think that a good friend of mine is on the right track with her morning ritual. She starts her day by giving herself a big hug, kissing both shoulders, and saying, "Not bad for a ..." I won't share her descriptor. Create your own. In this one instance, the phrase might be disparaging – it's okay. Sometimes, repeating a negative phrase reminds you that it has no real meaning and you're above it. I might say, "Not bad for a short, overweight old lady." That's who I see in the mirror and I'm damned proud of her.

Project a positive image. That's what people will see. Show your strength. I have a friend – female – who is under five feet tall and with one stare and a shift in tone can command any classroom full of rowdy adolescents. She projects power in a way they can't question. You can do it too.

Track your accomplishments, large and small. Showcase your abilities every chance you get. Spend time with people who believe in you. At a recent conference I was in conversation with a woman who was busy telling me how brilliant she was and how I wasn't good enough to be on her podcast. I just shrugged and said, "Well, you never know" and was rewarded by the third woman in the conversation, a well-known expert and author with a nationally syndicated podcast, immediately announcing that I would be on her podcast.

One Final Word About Vision

Don't question your dreams and visions. Write them down and keep them nearby. Many of the serial careerists I've interviewed did this. One envisioned both her husband and safaris to Africa. She got both. Somehow, seemingly without any effort on their part, these dreams became reality. I think that the late Wayne Dyer captured this best in the title of one of his many personal development books – *You'll See It When You Believe It*.

Two friends of mine had similar experiences when searching for their next home. One had been carrying with her a picture of the exact kitchen in her new home. The other opened her search portfolio and realized that she was looking out of the window of an apartment at exactly the view depicted in a picture in her hand.

Visioning keeps your vision in the forefront. It opens doors that you might otherwise never have seen.

So, I've given you a lot to absorb. This isn't a one-and-done process. This is a roadmap to building and maintaining a life you will love. I hope that your hard copy becomes dogeared, underscored, and tattered. I hope that your digital copy is full of bookmarks and highlights. There's always more to know, though. With that in mind, knowing that there are far too many resources for anyone to sort through, I'm ending by visualizing your incredible serial career and offering a list of some of my favorite resources.

Resources (in no particular order):

Not Done Yet!: How Women Over 50 Regain Their Confidence and Claim Workplace Power, Bonnie Marcus

This is a great motivational book for anyone who feels that they're too old. It includes valuable information about how to fight bias and discrimination.

What Color Is Your Parachute? 2022: Your Guide to a Lifetime of Meaningful Work and Career Success, Richard N. Bolles and Katharine Brooks, Ed.D

One of the first career-search books, this has been a comprehensive guide since 1970. It's updated regularly. I've been recommending it since the first edition.

Big Wild Love: The Unstoppable Power of Letting Go, Jill Sherer Murray

How to let go of bad relationships to create a joyous life.

You'll See It When You Believe It: The Way to Your Personal Transformation, Wayne Dyer

One of my favorite guides to personal transformation and one of many excellent books by Wayne Dyer.

The Success Principles: How to Get from Where You Are to Where You Want to Be, Jack Canfield

This step-by-step guide helps you overcome obstacles and take action. His reminder that **E**vent + **R**esponse = **O**utcome has changed millions of lives. As a licensed graduate of his training program, I have found this seemingly simple reminder invaluable

The Energy of Money, Maria Nemeth, Ph.D

Excellent guide to understanding your relationship to money and managing your finances.

Bird By Bird: Some Instruction on Writing and Life, Anne Lamott

My personal favorite writer's guide. I gave copies to all my dissertation advisees and still give copies to aspiring writers.

For more information about creating or managing your serial career, including occasional mailings with tips and updates and group and individual coaching, you can reach me at: www. susanrmeyer.com

Acknowledgements

This project grew out of my coaching practice, my graduate studies, and my many interviews with women. I'm grateful to all of the people who let me into their lives over the past thirty years. Each one was my teacher and each had an amazing story. I'm especially indebted to Gloria, my first interview, and the women of Medgar Evers College who contributed their life stories to my dissertation study.

Cheryl Benton, the brilliant creator of The Three Tomatoes and Three Tomatoes Publishing, is a joy to work with. She's a gifted editor, an astute businesswoman, a creative genius, and a wonderful friend. Her support, knowledge, and attention to detail made this book possible.

The supporting cast that kept me going during the writing process includes many of the faculty and students at the Story Summit Writing School. I'm especially grateful to Amy Ferris, whose New York City workshops got me writing again and whose ongoing support helped me know what was possible. During the summer of 2021, a Story Summit course called "Get It Finished" gave me a tribe, a deadline, and an incredible support group that included Mary Cyrns (aka Melody Writes), Tana Macpherson-Smith, Denise Marinez, and Jane Claire Purden. Denise was an outstanding accountability partner and I loved our daily texts.

The "Her Spirit" retreat gave me a group of supportive sisters, good advice, and suggestions. I am deeply indebted to Lori Sokol, publisher of Women's eNews, who contributed the book's title.

My beta readers – Isora Bosch, Marsha Lehman, and Karen Burd – were invaluable. They untangled the messy sequence that was my first draft, suggested additions, and helped me set the tone I wanted.

I want to thank a few of The Three Tomatoes Zoom cocktail group – Francene Katzman, Randie Levine Miller, Margot Tohn, and Beatty Cohan – for selecting the best draft cover design.

Finally, I couldn't have done this without the ongoing support of my Spirit Sisters: Marsha Lehman, Deborah Roth, Siobhan Murphy, Maggie Lichtenberg, and Grace Dufree.

Dr. Susan R. Meyer

About the Author

Dr. Susan R. Meyer knows how to help people create the life they want and has spent decades working with women and men who want to create a clear path to success. Whether you're looking for a totally different path or simply want to tweak your career trajectory, her extensive experience in life, career, and transition coaching will help you take an informed look at your own life and build on what's revealed. Susan brings an eclectic background to her practice. Her skills in getting to the heart of issues and working with clients to craft clear plans grew out of years of coaching, teaching (preschool through grad school), and training (trainers and line staff through executive managers). This experience set allows her to see the common themes in each client's experience and use those to develop individualized strategies.

Her book *Fifty Over Fifty: Wise and Wild Women Creating Wonderful Lives (And You Can Too!)* tells the stories of fifty amazing women who have created exciting life paths and served as an inspiration for this book.

Susan's background includes designing and leading programs on topics including emotional intelligence, leadership development, reflective mentoring, team building, visual problem-solving, fierce communication, career development, life planning, strategic learning, coaching skills for leaders, performance management, and the personal growth workshop, Women Living for Today and Tomorrow, featured in *The New York Times*.

Made in United States
North Haven, CT
26 February 2022

16524181R00109